new vegetarian

celia brooks brown

photography by philip webb

new vegetarian

bold and beautiful recipes for every occasion

RYLAND
PETERS
& SMALL

LONDON NEW YORK

Senior Designer	Paul Tilby
Commissioning Editor	Elsa Petersen-Schepelern
Editor	Maddalena Bastianelli
Production	Meryl Silbert
Art Director	Gabriella Le Grazie
Publishing Director	Alison Starling
Food Stylist	Celia Brooks Brown
Food Stylist's Assistant	Kate Habershon
Stylist	Malena Burgess

First published in the USA in 2001
by Ryland Peters & Small, Inc.
519 Broadway, 5th Floor
New York, NY 10012
www.rylandpeters.com

This paperback edition first published in 2005

10 9 8 7 6 5 4 3 2

Library of Congress Cataloging-in-Publication Data

Brown, Celia Brooks.
    New vegetarian : bold and beautiful recipes for
every occasion / Celia Brooks Brown ; photography
by Philip Webb.
        p. cm.
    Includes bibliographical references and index.
    ISBN 978-1-84172-984-8 (pbk.)
    1. Vegetarian cookery. 2. Cookery,
International. I. Title.
    TX837.B8398 2005
    641.5'636--dc22

2005005633

Printed in China.

for Mom

AUTHOR ACKNOWLEDGMENTS

I am deeply grateful to Eric Treuille and the team at Books for Cooks for their infinite
support and encouragement. Huge thanks to Elsa and Maddie for their hard work
and stoic patience. Much heartfelt gratitude to Philip Webb for creating such
vivacious pictures, and to Kate Habershon, Lizzie Harris, Paul Tilby, and Sarah Cuttle
for making the photo shoot such brilliant fun. I extend warm appreciation to all
who participated in my home tastings (and endured a cold, dark barbecue in
February)—Fisher, Ben, Callum, Alex, Sarah, Jessica, James, Sarah W., Tarda,
Mark J., Dom, Julia, Paula, Paulie, and Steve M.—and to my gorgeous husband
Dan for telling it like it is.

Thanks also to Michael van Straten for nutritional advice and The Vegetarian Society
(www.vegsoc.org) for invaluable information.

NOTES

All spoon measurements are level unless otherwise stated.

All fruits and vegetables should be washed thoroughly and peeled, unless otherwise
stated. Unwaxed citrus fruits should be used whenever possible.

Outdoor grills, ovens, and broilers should be preheated to the required temperature—if
you are using a convection oven, cooking times should be reduced according to the
manufacturer's instructions.

Asian ingredients are available in gourmet stores and certain large supermarkets,
as well as Asian stores.

contents

introduction

Welcome to the new era of vegetarian cooking and eating! It's food for a dynamic life through a healthy diet—and food for the sheer enjoyment of it. It's food modeled on ancient world cuisines, as well as fusing the myriad of modern ingredients available to us today.

Every day, more people are deciding to eat less meat or are giving it up altogether. Cooking vegetarian can require a little more creativity than cooking with meat, but that doesn't mean it has to be complicated. This book aims to inspire both the seasoned cook and the novice, too.

New vegetarian cooking and eating is not about finding substitutes for meat, but rather about shifting the focus. Instead of the conventional "meat and two vegetables," meals without meat should be a varied composition of texture, color, and flavor. Imagine a plate of mezze—creamy hummus singing with garlic, olives twinkling like jewels, smoky grilled vegetables, and grains dressed in fresh lemon juice and peppery olive oil—and a warm and soft pocket of pillowy flatbread to scoop it all up. Do you miss the meat?

BEING VEGETARIAN

There are many reasons for being vegetarian and even if you aren't one, you probably know someone who is. Some of the most common reasons for being vegetarian or cutting down on meat are:

- You may want a healthy diet to give you a greater sense of well-being.
- You may boycott meat because you don't agree with the animal husbandry methods used in the meat and poultry industries.
- You may have environmental concerns.
- You may have religious reasons.
- You may, like me, have a natural dislike for, or indifference towards meat.

Whatever the reason, the health benefits are clear. The World Health Organization recommends a diet that is low in saturated animal fats and high in complex carbohydrates, as found in fruits, vegetables, grains, and legumes—typical of many vegetarian diets. Organizations such as the American Dietetic Association claim that vegetarians may be less likely to develop heart disease, high blood pressure, certain forms of cancer, and many other health problems.

All the reasons for living without meat are good ones. Just remember, no one likes a preaching vegetarian. Celebrate being a vegetarian for the positive reasons, and enjoy a life of cooking and eating truly good food.

BUY FRESH, SEASONAL, AND, IF POSSIBLE, ORGANIC

The fruits of the earth are the main elements of vegetarian eating. Everyone has a built-in self-defense mechanism which makes us sensitive to food that might be harmful to us—it smells odd, looks discolored, lacks luster. But foods can deceive us—a bag of perky supermarket salad may look fresh, but why? Why are February greenhouse tomatoes tasteless spheres? Fresh produce is delicate, so it is usually treated—with preservatives, wax, gas, or irradiation—to sustain its long journey to the supermarket shelves. By purchasing food in season and from as local a source as possible—such as farmers' markets—you'll get fresher, purer produce. The impact on the environment will be less too, as thousands of gallons of airline fuel and diesel go into transporting out-of-season produce across vast distances.

The use of toxic pesticides and artificial fertilizers in the intensive farming of crops does increase productivity, and has shaped the evolution of modern agriculture—but this has had unfortunate consequences. Quality and flavor are compromised by rapid production, toxic residues end up in our food, and the environment becomes polluted. The best way to be absolutely certain that your food is safe and additive-free is to buy certified organic ingredients. It means spending a little more money, but it's worth it for flavor, health, and peace of mind.

The issue of genetically modified or GM foods is another concern. Genetic modification involves the insertion of a gene from one species into another. The aim is to make life easier for the producer, but what about the consumer? It is not yet known what the long-term effects of consuming GM foods will be, nor what effect GM will have on the environment. A soybean plant engineered to resist herbicide can then be sprayed liberally with toxic, non-biodegradable chemicals that end up in the food chain—and ultimately on our plates. Buying organic is one way to avoid GM products, and even then there's some risk.

RELAX AND ENJOY!

Remember, ultimately food is fun. If you can spend time shopping and sourcing the best ingredients, it can be hugely rewarding, especially when you come to eat it.

When we get stressed or worried about cooking, it never seems to taste as good. But don't think of cooking as a chore—it can be very relaxing. Read the recipe carefully and, if you think you can make it, try it. As your confidence grows, you'll find that the satisfaction in the end result is much greater than the effort you put in. Eventually you will want to play around with the recipes and add your own special touches. When you see cooking as a creative process, you can use it to express yourself, as a way to enjoy yourself and please others.

Be brave, be adventurous! But bear in mind that some immortally classic combinations, like pesto for example, are not necessarily improved by substituting, say, lemongrass and Roquefort for basil and Parmesan. Within the boundaries of tradition and sound judgement, there is room for individual expression. Your cooking style is based on who you are, and what you like to eat. Interestingly, many professional chefs still cite their mothers as the best cooks they know.

health notes

without meat, what are we missing out on?

When I tell someone I'm a vegetarian, I often get a reaction of concern—"It must be so difficult to make sure you have a balanced diet," or "Isn't it hard to get enough protein?" The truth is that all the nutrients you need are abundant in vegetarian food. It's just important to eat a varied diet and to understand some basic nutrition facts.

PROTEIN

Protein is an essential part of the diet, but by cutting out meat, you're not in danger of being deprived of protein, unless you plan to live on leaves alone! Grains, legumes, eggs, and dairy produce are all good sources of protein. Protein should make up only 15 percent of the diet so, provided your diet is varied, you will get enough. Try not to rely exclusively on cheese and eggs for protein—they're high in saturated fat which is linked to heart disease, and so should be eaten in moderation.

Proteins are made up of amino acids, of which there are 22 in all. The body manufactures most of these, but eight of them have to be acquired from the diet. Meat, fish, eggs, and dairy produce contain all eight (they are "complete proteins"), but soybeans* are the only non-animal complete protein source—one reason why tofu is such a prized vegetarian food. Rice, grains, legumes, and nuts do not contain all eight, but by mixing these foods in the daily diet, for example, rice with beans, or peanut butter with bread, we make up complete proteins. Recent research shows that these complementary proteins do not have to be eaten together, as the body stores the amino acids short-term.

*Recent research suggests that eating large quantities of soy products can be harmful. As with eggs and cheese, it's best eaten in moderation. Fermentation may reduce harmful effects; so fermented soy products such as soy sauce, tempeh, and miso are thought to be safer.

IRON

Iron plays an essential role in the circulatory system. It is used by the body to manufacture haemoglobin in your blood, which carries oxygen from the lungs to all the tissue cells and major organs in your body. Vitamin C, found in fresh fruit and vegetables, increases iron absorption.

Spinach, though it may have worked wonders for Popeye, is not a good source of iron. It does have a high iron content, but this is cancelled out by a high content of oxalic acid that binds with the iron to form an insoluble substance.

OTHER MINERALS

Meat and fish supply other essential minerals, especially calcium, zinc, selenium, and iodine. Happily all are abundant in vegetarian foods.

B VITAMINS

B vitamins are essential for maintaining a healthy digestive and nervous system. Common food sources include yeast, whole-grain cereals, nuts, green vegetables, and legumes.

B12 is the only B vitamin that doesn't occur in plant foods (except seaweed). Only a very small amount is needed for good health and it can be found in eggs and dairy products. If you are a vegan, you should take this vitamin in supplement form, or incorporate B12-enriched foods into the diet.

OTHER VITAMINS

Vitamin D and Vitamin A are common in meat and fish as well as vegetarian foods. We make our own vitamin D when we are exposed to the sun. We get it from dairy products as well. Vitamin D, however, is not present in plant foods, so vegans are advised to take supplements.

Vitamin A is also found in dairy products, but the body also converts beta-carotene, found in orange-fleshed and dark green vegetables, into this essential vitamin.

OTHER ELEMENTS OF A HEALTHY DIET

Carbohydrate, fiber, and fat are also essential to the diet on a daily basis.

The body converts carbohydrate into energy. The two main types of carbohydrate are starches and sugars. Starches are found in plant-based foods such as

rice, bread, potatoes, pasta, cereals, and legumes. The unrefined types, such as whole wheat bread and brown rice, are the most valuable to the body, as they are rich in fiber and B vitamins.

Sugars which occur naturally in fruit and vegetables (as opposed to a jelly doughnut) are valuable energy and fiber sources as well. These foods contain a whole range of other essential nutrients, and should form a major part of everyday eating.

A moderate amount of fat is essential too—vegetable fats tend to be more unsaturated, which is a more healthy type of fat, than animal fats, which tend to be saturated (this includes cheese and eggs).

VEGETARIAN DAILY DIET

Doctors and vegetarian organizations recommend a daily diet for vegetarians which should include:

- 3 or 4 servings of cereals or potatoes
- 4 or 5 servings of fruit and vegetables (though most nutritionists would recommend 5 to 6 servings)
- 2 to 3 servings of legumes, nuts, and seeds
- 2 servings of milk, cheese, eggs, or soy products.

- A small amount of vegetable oil and butter.
- Some yeast extracts, fortified with vitamin B12.

BEING VEGAN

Being a vegan means not consuming any animal by-products of any kind such as eggs, butter and milk—even honey. And it's not just about food. Vegans will not wear leather or anything else derived from animals. There are a surprisingly large number of everyday items which may use animal products as an ingredient or in the manufacturing process, including moisturizers, chewing gum, wine, beer, toothpaste, and laundry detergent.

Vegans can still share the health benefits of a vegetarian diet despite these restrictions. However, it takes a lot more effort and consideration because there is a risk of malnutrition, especially vitamin B12 deficiency.

If you are considering becoming vegan, find out more about veganism first, and seek the advice of a nutritionist or dietician.

the basics

RICE Long grain or short grain, rice is a traditional vegetarian staple and is amazingly convenient. My favorite is basmati, which has a lovely, nutty flavor and cooks in just 10–12 minutes in boiling salted water. Other varieties include white long grain and Thai fragrant rice. Italian risotto rice and Japanese sushi rice are all short grain. Converted rice is also available: the grains have been steam-treated to drive the nutrients back into the grain. Brown rice, also known as wholegrain rice, is not milled (only the husk from the grain is removed). It takes 30–45 minutes to cook, has a nutty flavor and is high in B-vitamins and fiber. Rice should always be measured by volume and not by weight and cooked in twice the volume of liquid.

COUSCOUS Not to be confused with a grain, couscous is in fact a type of wheat pasta. It is delicious cold in salads or served hot with vegetable stews. It is easy to prepare: simply pour boiling water or stock over the couscous to cover, add a pinch of salt, and let stand for 10–15 minutes until the liquid is absorbed. Alternatively, steam or microwave, then add a little butter. Fluff the grains with a fork.

BULGUR Also known as cracked wheat, bulgur is probably best-known for its use in tabbouleh, a famous Lebanese dish. Bulgur is a good source of carbohydrate and will add bulk to vegetable dishes. Prepare in the same way as couscous, but let stand for 30 minutes.

POLENTA (CORNMEAL) Made from corn, which is ground to a fine or coarse meal. It is fabulous with butter and Parmesan cheese, served soft or set and cut into pieces, then pan-grilled or fried. Do not use the variety that takes only 5 minutes to cook or the ready-made polenta that is vacuum-packed. Both lack flavor and nuance. Polenta (uncooked) can used like breadcrumbs to give a crisp, crunchy coating to food (page 50). For cooking instructions for polenta, see page 72.

TOFU Made from soybeans, tofu (bean curd) is the best protein alternative to meat. Because it has no taste, tofu is usually marinated with strong, assertive flavors, such as garlic, ginger, and chiles, and either stir-fried or roasted. There are two types of tofu: silken tofu, which is soft and smooth, used mainly in shakes, cheesecakes, and cakes, and firm tofu, which has a more robust texture, suitable for stir-frying, deep-frying, and roasting. Firm tofu is also available smoked, but it doesn't need to be marinated, although it can taste artificial. Tofu will not keep long: if it smells sour, don't use it. If you don't use all the tofu at once, put the remainder in a bowl, cover with cold water, refrigerate, and use within 2 days, changing the water at least once.

Tempeh is another protein-rich food. Made from fermented soybeans, it has a firm texture, good flavor, and can be fried, sautéed, broiled, or roasted. It is usually available frozen from natural food stores.

EGGPLANT A very versatile vegetable, eggplant can be stuffed, roasted, char-grilled, fried, or added to rice and pasta dishes, stews, and bakes. Sprinkling eggplant with salt is a traditional technique used to draw out any bitter juices. However, if you buy the modern, non-bitter variety you do not need to do this. But if you plan to sauté eggplant in oil, you may want to add a pinch of salt—it firms up the flesh so that less oil will be absorbed. Salt will also make the eggplant crisper. Resist the temptation to add more oil, because some of the already absorbed oil will be released back into the pan as the eggplant cooks.

CHILES The intense fiery heat of chiles comes from capsaicin, a chemical that is present in varying degrees in all parts of the chile. It is strongest in the membranes and the seeds, so take care when seeding chiles. Wash your hands thoroughly afterwards and take particular care not to touch your eyes—capsaicin can sting. (I always wear rubber gloves when handling chiles.) Chiles are used extensively in Thai and Mexican cooking. As a general rule, green chiles are milder than red ones and the smaller the chile, the hotter it is. There are a few exceptions; the habañero and Scotch bonnet are both large, rippled, and lantern-shaped, and often red, yellow, or orange. Both are best avoided unless you really want to hit the ceiling.

OLIVE OIL Try to use the best extra virgin olive oil you can afford. A wildly expensive estate oil may be wasted in cooking—almost good enough to drink, it should be used in the raw for salads and dunking bread. Like wines, olive oils have different characteristics of fruitiness and pepperiness, and what you love is an individual matter.

COOKING WITH WINE A splash of wine is a welcome addition to many recipes. The only rule of thumb is not to add it at the end of cooking, but at the start, to give the alcohol at least a few minutes to evaporate. My favorites are:

- Madeira (from the island bearing its name) is sweet and nutty—keep a bottle by the stove at all times.
- Port is a fortified wine and in cooking it imparts a deep wine flavor and dark color.
- Vermouth isn't the finest of drinks, except as part of a dry martini, though it is the best fortified white wine for risotto. It can be substituted wherever white wine is required, as it doesn't oxidize and can be kept ready and waiting for splashing.
- Slightly less common are the two Japanese rice wines; mirin, a sweet wine for cooking only, and sake. Both, especially in combination, are wonderful in stir-fries and marinades.

BREADCRUMBS Store-bought breadcrumbs taste stale and are generally bad value. Some bakeries will sell you a cheap bag of crumbs, but you can easily make your own by pulverizing stale cubes of bread in the food processor. You can then freeze them in bags. If you haven't got any stale bread, buy a couple of crusty rolls or a small baguette, slice in half, and toast in the oven until crisp. Break into pieces and process in the machine.

basic recipes

vegetable stock

Using homemade vegetable stock creates a depth of flavor in soups and it is well worth going to the trouble of making. In fact, it's no trouble at all—just boil up a pan of water and pop in a quartered onion, sliced celery with leaves, a sliced carrot, some parsley, and salt and simmer for 30 minutes. And there you have it. But you needn't buy vegetables specifically for stock. Always save the water you've used to steam, blanch, or boil vegetables: cool and store in a sealed bag in the freezer and you'll always have some to hand. Alternatively, boil up vegetable off-cuts. Stock options—good and bad—are:

- Especially good: scallion and leek greens (well washed), broccoli and cauliflower stems, celery leaves, fresh pea pods, herb stems, fennel tops, tomato skins.
- Not so good: onion skins, cabbage leaves, potato, bell pepper seeds.

I have to admit I regularly succumb to the convenience of bouillon cubes or granules. Read the label and go organic or without "flavorings" or additives.

beans

Freshly cooked beans do taste better than canned, but not always infinitely superior. While it's hardly back-breaking to throw some dried beans in a bowl of water and leave them overnight, it does require a little forward planning and possibly takes away a little of the spontaneity. So I've given both options in the recipes. If you are using dried beans, remember:

- Lentils DO NOT need soaking, but should be rinsed before cooking.
- Rinse beans first and check for pebbles or imperfect beans.
- Put the beans in a bowl with 3 times their volume of cold water. Leave 12 hours or overnight (in the refrigerator if it's warm in the kitchen).
- Drain off the soaking water and boil the beans in plenty of fresh water. Let them boil furiously for 10 minutes, then add salt. (Adding salt before this will toughen the skins.)
- Skim off any foam that forms on the surface of the water.
- Beans will cook in between 30 minutes and 2 hours, depending on the type of bean and its age.

basic tomato sauce

2 tablespoons olive oil

1 onion, chopped

3 garlic cloves, chopped

16 oz. canned chopped tomatoes

1 teaspoon balsamic vinegar

1 teaspoon sugar

salt and pepper

Heat the oil in a skillet. Add the onion and sauté gently until translucent. Add garlic and sauté until fragrant. Add the remaining ingredients and simmer gently for 15–20 minutes.

Optional extras: 1 chopped serrano chile (added with the onion), a splash of red wine, Madeira, port, or vermouth (added with tomatoes), or fresh torn basil leaves (added in the last minute of cooking).

basic cheese sauce

2 tablespoons butter

2 tablespoons all-purpose flour

1¼ cups milk

1 cup grated sharp-flavored hard cheese such as Cheddar, Monterey Jack, or Gruyère

Melt the butter in a skillet set over a low heat. Sprinkle with the flour.

Cook, stirring, for 2 minutes, to burst the starch grains. Meanwhile warm the milk in the microwave or in a separate saucepan. Gradually pour the warmed milk into the flour mixture, stirring constantly. When thickened, stir in the grated cheese and stir until smooth. Serve immediately.

Optional extras: Infuse the milk by simmering it for a few minutes with a bay leaf, half a sliced onion, and a garlic clove.
At the same time as the cheese, add 2 teaspoons Dijon mustard or 2 teaspoons horseradish.

pesto

a large bunch of basil

1 cup pine nuts, lightly toasted in a dry skillet

2 garlic cloves

½ cup grated Parmesan cheese

⅓ cup olive oil

kosher salt and freshly ground black pepper

Put the basil, pine nuts, garlic, and Parmesan in a food processor and blend. Drizzle in the olive oil little by little. Season to taste.

Optional extras: pesto is one of those sublime combinations that

really shouldn't be interfered with. An exception is Smoked Chile Pesto, made with chipotle and pimentón—pimentón is smoked paprika, but if you can't find it, use ordinary paprika. Before processing, soak 1 chipotle in hot water, remove the seeds, and chop the flesh. Add to the pesto, with 2 teaspoons mild pimentón, before processing.

basic vinaigrette

It's a matter of personal taste, but I use a ratio of 3 parts olive oil to 1 part balsamic, cider, or wine vinegar. Using a mortar and pestle, mash 1 garlic clove and 1 teaspoon coarse salt to a smooth purée. Whisk in 2 tablespoons vinegar, pepper, and a little sugar. Gradually whisk in 3 tablespoons olive oil until well emulsified.

Alternatively, crush the garlic clove and shake all the ingredients in a screw-top jar.

Optional extras: add 1–2 teaspoons mustard and ½ teaspoon dried herbs de Provence or a small handful of fresh chopped herbs, especially dill. Alternatively, use lemon juice instead of vinegar.

guacamole

2 very ripe avocados

juice of 1 lime

kosher salt or sea salt

Scoop the flesh from the avocados into a bowl. Add lime juice and salt and mash with a fork or potato masher. If made ahead of time, reserve 1 avocado stone and leave it in the guacamole until time to serve. Miraculously, it will stop the guacamole discoloring.

Optional extras: Add 1 crushed garlic clove, 1 chopped chile or a few dashes Tabasco sauce, 1 small, finely chopped onion, 1 chopped tomato, and a small bunch of cilantro, chopped.

the vegetarian pantry

THE FOLLOWING ITEMS, MOST USED IN THIS BOOK, ARE ALL USEFUL TO HAVE ON HAND FOR VEGETARIAN COOKING.

OILS AND VINEGARS

extra virgin olive oil

sunflower oil

sesame oil

truffle oil (drizzle on all things mushroomy just before serving)

white and red wine vinegar

balsamic vinegar

cider vinegar

rice vinegar

sushi vinegar (makes a lovely light salad dressing on its own)

SEASONINGS AND FLAVORINGS

vegetable bouillon cubes or powder

coarse kosher salt or sea salt

fine kosher salt or sea salt (for baking)

Japanese soy sauce, tamari, or shoyu (fermented dark soy sauce)

light soy sauce

Thai sweet chile sauce

Tabasco sauce

chile paste, such as harissa or sambal oelek

vegetarian Worcestershire sauce

tamarind pulp

COOKING WINES

red, white, and Madeira

port (especially ruby port, as it's relatively inexpensive and has a deep color)

vermouth

mirin and sake (see Cooking with Wine, page 11)

NUTS AND SEEDS

sesame seeds

poppy seeds

pumpkin seeds

pine nuts

salted, roasted peanuts

slivered almonds

vacuum-packed chestnuts

PICKLES AND DRIED ITEMS

dried fruits such as raisins, golden raisins, apricots, cranberries, and prunes

pickled onions

capers in salt or vinegar

high-quality olives such as kalamata

pickled jalapeño pepper slices

dried smoked chiles, such as chipotles

dried porcini mushrooms

dried shiitake mushrooms

SPREADS, SAUCES, AND SWEET THINGS

honey

light corn syrup

vanilla extract

rose water

orange blossom water

marmalade

berry, plum, or apricot preserves

lemon or orange curd

peanut butter

unsweetened cocoa powder

vegetarian gelatin alternative

sugar: superfine, soft brown, and confectioner's sugar

BAKING, PASTA, GRAINS, AND LEGUMES

all-purpose flour

bread flour

baking powder

baking soda

wheat germ

masa harina

cornstarch

polenta (cornmeal)

rolled oats

rice: basmati, arborio (for risotto), and sushi rice

bulgur

pasta

couscous

noodles: rice stick, rice vermicelli, egg noodles

flour tortillas

lentils (especially Puy)

dried beans

FOOD IN CANS

refried beans

chickpeas

lima beans

pinto or cannellini beans

corn kernels

coconut milk

coconut cream

peeled plum tomatoes

chopped tomatoes

HERBS AND SPICES

bay leaves

oregano

saffron strands

ground turmeric

mild chili powder (generally a mix with garlic, cumin, and oregano)

cayenne pepper

hot pepper flakes

paprika

pimentón (smoked paprika)

cloves: ground and whole

cinnamon: ground and sticks or bark

whole nutmegs

vanilla beans

cumin: ground and seeds

coriander seeds

cardamom pods

whole fenugreek

sumac (deep red, citrus-flavored spice, excellent sprinkled on salad)

MISCELLANEOUS

mayonnaise

mustard: English, Dijon, wholegrain

creamed horseradish

kitchen equipment

chef's knife and sharpener—buy a large chef's knife. The best are made from high-carbon steel. They have a razor-sharp edge which will need sharpening regularly.

vegetable paring knife

bread knife

food processor with chopping blade, slicing blade and grater.

blender

stick blender (immersion blender) for puréeing soups.

balloon whisk or hand-held mixer

large wok with dome lid—indispensable, not only for stir-frying, but also deep-frying and steaming. Traditional woks, made from iron or carbon steel with a wooden handle (a design perfected over 2000 years ago), are rounded on the bottom, and therefore only suitable for cooking over a gas flame. If your heat source is electric or another fuel, such as oil or wood, opt for a modern version with a partly flat base.

To season a new traditional wok, scrub well, rinse and dry. Wipe with vegetable oil and place over a low flame for 10 minutes. Cool, wipe away the burnt film, and repeat the process until it wipes clean. Never scrub when washing, but wipe clean with hot water and a sponge, and rub with vegetable oil after drying. If the wok does get scrubbed or becomes rusty, simply season again.

wok scoop—a shovel-like implement, ideal for stir-frying.

long tongs

spatula

potato masher

bamboo steamer—can be used in the wok or on top of a pan. These are very cheap and will need replacing every so often, as they absorb flavors.

bamboo or wire strainer or flat slotted spoon

large skillet—either nonstick or well-seasoned cast-iron—about 12 inches diameter.

heavy-bottom saucepans in a variety of sizes.

large heavy-duty stove-top grill pan—if you can find one that fits over two gas burners, so much the better.

large mortar and pestle

muffin pans—I have discovered a remarkable silicon-based rubberized Llorente muffin maker which eliminates the need for greasing. It makes 6 plump muffins that just pop out. Sold in stores such as Wal*Mart; KMart; Bed, Bath, & Beyond; and BJ's—or visit www.directlytoyou.com.

springform cake pan—9- or 10-inch diameter, 3 inches deep (springform pans have removable base and sides).

loaf pan—9 x 5 x 3 inch, standard size.

large and medium baking sheets

power shake

We must eat and drink to "break" the "fast" since last night's dinner. However, many of us don't even wake up hungry, or we're too busy getting ready for work or feeding the family. It's likely we'll put off eating until late morning, when our stomachs rumble loudly and we reach for a delicious but unhealthy sweet pastry. Instead, spare just five minutes in the morning to make a nutritious, filling shake to kick-start your day.

about 1 cup prepared fruit, such as berries, mango, banana, papaya, peach, apricot, melon, or kiwifruit

1 cup low-fat plain yogurt

1 cup fruit juice, such as orange, apple, pineapple, or cranberry

½ cup slivered almonds

2 tablespoons honey

3–4 tablespoons wheat germ

a pinch of ground cinnamon

SERVES 2

Put all the ingredients in a blender and blend until smooth. Pour into glasses and serve with a straw. This shake will keep in the refrigerator for 2 days.

VARIATIONS

- Use ½ cup silken tofu instead of the almonds.

- Replace the fruit juice with low-fat milk, soy milk, or unsweetened coconut milk.

- Omit the wheat germ and use rolled oats instead.

- Add other flavorings before blending, such as 1 teaspoon pure vanilla extract, a dash of almond extract, or 2 teaspoons grated fresh ginger.

- For a thick shake, add ice cubes before blending.

muffins

Nothing beats a fresh batch of home-baked muffins for an extra-special treat (with butter if you dare) and a cup of steaming coffee or tea. Though they're best eaten hot from the oven, the muffins can be made the night before, cooled, stored in an airtight container, then reheated before serving.

lemon poppy seed muffins

2 cups all-purpose flour

1 teaspoon baking powder

¼ teaspoon salt

3 tablespoons poppy seeds

1 cup sugar

2 eggs, lightly beaten

grated zest of 2 lemons and juice of 1

6 tablespoons butter, melted, or sunflower oil

1 teaspoon pure vanilla extract

½ cup low-fat plain yogurt

a large 6-cup or small 12-cup muffin pan, well greased

MAKES 6 LARGE OR 12 SMALL MUFFINS

Sift the flour and baking powder into a bowl and stir in the salt and poppy seeds. Add the remaining ingredients and fold everything together until just blended; do not beat or overmix. Spoon the batter into the prepared pan and bake in a preheated oven at 350°F for 20–30 minutes, until golden and firm. Let cool in the pan for 10 minutes, then invert onto a wire rack.

VARIATIONS

- Blueberry Muffins: omit the poppy seeds, lemon zest, and juice. Fold 1½ cups blueberries into the batter.

- Fruit and Nut Muffins: omit the poppy seeds, lemon zest, and juice. Add ½ cup dried mixed fruit and ½ cup chopped nuts to the batter.

corn muffins

½ cup all-purpose flour

2 teaspoons baking powder

1 teaspoon salt

2 cups coarse polenta or yellow cornmeal

½ cup sugar

2 eggs, lightly beaten

1 stick butter, melted

¾ cup milk

1 cup fresh corn kernels, or frozen and thawed

a large cup or small 12-cup muffin pan, well greased

MAKES 6 LARGE OR 12 SMALL MUFFINS

Heat the prepared pan in a preheated oven at 375°F for 5 minutes, make the outside of the muffins crisp). Sift the flour and baking powder into a bowl and stir in the salt, polenta or cornmeal, and sugar. Add the eggs, melted butter, and milk and mix until smooth. Add the corn and mix. Spoon the batter into the hot muffin pan and bake at the same temperature for 20–30 minutes, until golden and firm. Let cool in the pan for 10 minutes, then invert onto a wire rack.

VARIATION

- Chile Corn Muffins: reduce the sugar to 1 tablespoon. Add 1 teaspoon chopped serrano chile or 1 cup chopped red bell peppers.

A stack of fluffy, homemade pancakes in the morning will keep you fueled for hours. Make it before bedtime and leave it overnight in the refrigerator. In the morning, you'll have a breakfast feast in minutes.

pancakes

1½ cups all-purpose flour

2 teaspoons baking powder

1 teaspoon salt

3 tablespoons sugar

1 cup milk

2 eggs, lightly beaten

4 tablespoons unsalted butter, melted, plus extra for cooking

MAPLE BUTTER SYRUP

⅓ cup maple syrup

2 tablespoons unsalted butter

MAKES 8–12, SERVES 4

Sift the flour, baking powder, salt, and sugar into a bowl. Mix the milk, eggs, and the 4 tablespoons melted butter in a large pitcher, then add the flour mixture and mix quickly to make a batter (don't worry about lumps—they're good). Alternatively, make the batter in a bowl and transfer to a pitcher.

Heat a cast-iron skillet or flat-surfaced griddle until medium hot, grease lightly with extra butter, and pour in the batter in batches to make rounds, 3–4 inches in diameter. Cook for 1–2 minutes or until bubbles form on top of the pancakes and the underside is golden, then flip each one over and cook for 1 minute. Keep the pancakes warm in the oven while you cook the remaining batches.

Heat the maple syrup and butter together in a small saucepan or microwave, then stack the pancakes on warmed plates and pour over the buttery syrup.

COTTAGE CHEESE PANCAKES

Make the batter as above, then stir in ½ cup of cottage cheese. Proceed with the recipe. Serve with fresh berries, cherry or blackcurrant jelly, and sour cream, crème fraîche, or thick yogurt.

A favorite dish from my home in Colorado. Assembling the burritos is quick and simple, and you can save extra time in the morning if you make the salsa the night before or use a good-quality ready-made salsa—perfect even for the sleepiest of cooks.

breakfast burrito

To make the burritos, put each tortilla on a large sheet of foil, spread with the mashed beans, and top with the cheese. Gather the foil and fold it at the top to seal, keeping the tortilla relatively flat. Put in a preheated oven at 400°F for 7–10 minutes, until the cheese has just melted and the beans and tortilla heated through, but not crisp.

Meanwhile, beat the eggs, milk, chili powder, oregano, salt, and pepper in a bowl. Heat the oil in a nonstick skillet, add the egg mixture, and cook, stirring frequently, until just set. Remove the burritos from the oven, open the foil package, and spoon the scrambled eggs on top. Reseal and keep them warm in the oven.

When ready to eat, unwrap the burritos on a plate and, using the foil to help, roll each one into a cylinder. Top with salsa, guacamole, and a spoonful of yogurt or sour cream.

4 large flour tortillas, 8 inches in diameter

16 oz. canned refried beans, or canned borlotti or pinto beans, rinsed, drained, and mashed

2 cups grated sharp Cheddar cheese

6 eggs

2 tablespoons milk

1 teaspoon mild chili powder

a pinch of dried oregano

1 tablespoon olive oil

kosher salt or sea salt and freshly ground black pepper

TO SERVE

Pickled Jalapeño Salsa or Salsa Fresca (page 62–3)

Guacamole (page 13)

plain yogurt or sour cream

SERVES 4

japanese omelet

This technique for making a very light omelet was shown to me by a Japanese friend. The end result is a delicate *millefeuille*—thin layers of egg, deeply flavored with shiitake mushrooms. This four-person omelet is perfect for brunch or a lazy weekend breakfast. If you are feeling particularly hungry, serve the omelet with broiled vine tomatoes, slices of ripe avocado, and slices of hot buttered toast—bliss.

6 fresh or dried shiitake
mushrooms

3 teaspoons vegetable oil

8 eggs

½ cup vegetable stock or
mushroom soaking liquid
(see method)

1–1½ tablespoons light soy sauce

1 tablespoon mirin (Japanese
sweet rice wine) or 1 teaspoon
sugar

10-inch nonstick skillet

SERVES 4

1 If using dried shiitakes, soak them in hot water for 30 minutes, then drain, reserving ½ cup of the soaking liquid. Finely slice the mushrooms. Heat 2 teaspoons of the oil in the skillet, add the mushrooms, and sauté for 2 minutes, until golden. Drain on paper towels and set aside.

2 Put the eggs, vegetable stock or mushroom liquid, soy sauce, and mirin or sugar in a pitcher and beat with a fork. Heat the skillet and add the remaining oil. Pour in enough egg mixture to cover the base of the skillet, swirling to coat.

3 Sprinkle with a few mushrooms, then cook until the egg is barely set, but not dry. Using a heatproof, non-metal spatula, loosen the edges and roll up the egg layer from one side of the pan to the other. Do not remove.

4 Pour in more egg mixture as before, letting it touch the rolled omelet. Add a few mushrooms and cook until the egg is barely set. Starting with the cooked omelet, roll it to the other side of the skillet—as you do this the new egg layer with roll up with it.

5 Repeat, layering and rolling until all the mushroom and egg mixture has been used. The finished omelet should be quite thick with many rolled layers.

6 Slide the omelet out of the skillet onto a large sheet of foil. Roll up into a long sausage shape and scrunch the foil at the ends to seal. Let stand 5–10 minutes.

7 Unwrap and remove the foil, then cut the omelet crosswise into 4 or 8 pieces and serve.

celery root, saffron, and orange soup **with parsley gremolata**

An elegant, rich soup, which can also be made dairy-free for vegans—use olive oil instead of butter and leave out the yogurt or crème fraîche. Although the parsley gremolata is optional, it will lift both color and flavor.

Heat the butter or oil in a saucepan, add the onion, and cook until softened. Add the celery root and potato, if using, cover, and cook for 10 minutes, stirring occasionally. Add the remaining ingredients. Bring to a boil and simmer for 20 minutes until the vegetables are tender. Using a hand-held stick immersion blender, purée until smooth. Alternatively, purée in a blender or food processor, in batches if necessary.

To make the gremolata, if using, put all the ingredients in a food processor or spice grinder and process until smooth. Alternatively, use a mortar and pestle.

To serve, ladle the soup into warmed bowls and spoon over the gremolata and sour cream or yogurt.

2 tablespoons butter or olive oil

1 large onion, chopped

1 celery root, about 1½ lb., peeled and cut into cubes (make up the weight with potatoes, if necessary)

4 cups vegetable stock

½ teaspoon saffron strands, lightly ground with a mortar and pestle

1 tablespoon honey

grated zest and juice of 1 large orange

kosher salt or sea salt and freshly ground black pepper

sour cream or plain yogurt, to serve

PARSLEY GREMOLATA (OPTIONAL)

1 garlic clove

1 teaspoon coarse kosher salt or sea salt

a handful of fresh flat-leaf parsley

2 tablespoons olive oil

SERVES 4

soups & salads

I've lost count of how many times I've been told, "this is the best gazpacho I've ever tasted." Ice-cold and enhanced with avocado, lime, cumin, and chile, this soup is refreshingly hard to beat on a hot summer's day. If you have the foresight, freeze cilantro leaves in ice cubes and use them to give your soup a decorative finish.

mexican gazpacho

2 garlic cloves

1 teaspoon coarse kosher salt or sea salt

1 large cucumber, peeled and coarsely chopped

1 yellow bell pepper, seeded and coarsely chopped

2 celery stalks, coarsely chopped

4 ripe tomatoes, coarsely chopped

1 red onion, coarsely chopped

4 cups fresh tomato juice

2 teaspoons cumin seeds, pan-toasted

1 teaspoon mild chili powder

1 ripe avocado, halved and pitted

juice of 2 limes

freshly ground black pepper

TO SERVE

cilantro leaves set in ice cubes, or chopped cilantro

SERVES 6

Using a mortar and pestle, pound the garlic with the salt until puréed. Put the cucumber, bell pepper, celery, tomatoes, and onion in a bowl, add the puréed garlic, and mix well. Transfer half of the mixture to a food processor and pulse until chopped but still slightly chunky. Pour into a bowl. Purée the remaining mixture until smooth, then add to the bowl. Mix in the tomato juice, cumin, chili powder, and freshly ground black pepper to taste.

Chill for several hours until very cold or overnight. If short of time, put the soup in the freezer for 30 minutes to chill.

Cut the avocado into small cubes, toss in the lime juice until well coated, then stir into the gazpacho.

To serve, ladle the soup into chilled bowls, then add a few ice cubes or sprinkle with chopped cilantro.

shiitake and portobello soup

with madeira and thyme

This soup is simplicity itself. There may seem to be a lot of mushrooms in it, but they shrink considerably when cooked and release their flavorful juices into the aromatic broth.

2 tablespoons butter

1 onion, chopped

2 garlic cloves, chopped

10 oz. shiitake mushrooms, torn or chopped into big chunks

10 oz. portobello or other large mushrooms, torn or chopped into big chunks

⅔ cup Madeira wine or dry sherry

2 cups vegetable stock

a bunch of fresh thyme, tied with kitchen twine

kosher salt or sea salt and freshly ground black pepper

TO SERVE

heavy cream

chopped parsley

freshly ground black pepper

SERVES 4

Melt the butter in a large saucepan, add the onion, and cook over a low heat until softened and translucent. Add the garlic, mushrooms, salt, and pepper. Increase the heat, cover, and cook, stirring occasionally, until the mushrooms have softened and their juices released, about 5 minutes.

Pour in the stock and Madeira or sherry and drop in the bundle of thyme. Bring to a boil, then cover and simmer for 15 minutes. Remove the thyme. Using a hand-held stick immersion blender, coarsely purée the mixture. Alternatively, purée in a blender or food processor, in batches if necessary. Ladle into warmed bowls, top with a swirl of cream, chopped parsley, and lots of black pepper, then serve.

lentil, coconut, and wilted spinach soup

Puy lentils are grown in France and have achieved a regal status among pulses. They have a distinctive flavor and, unlike other lentils, hold their shape well when cooked. If unavailable, use green or brown lentils. Add the spinach at the end: it doesn't need cooking.

⅔ cup Puy lentils

4 cups vegetable stock

1 onion, chopped

2 fat garlic cloves, chopped

2 teaspoons ground cumin

1 cup canned coconut milk

2–3 tablespoons dark soy sauce

4 small handfuls of baby spinach, about 2 cups

kosher salt and freshly ground black pepper

SERVES 4

Rinse the lentils, then put in a large saucepan and add enough cold water just to cover. Boil for 10 minutes, then add the remaining ingredients, except the spinach. Reduce the heat and simmer for 20–30 minutes or until the lentils are tender.

Put a small handful of the spinach in 4 warmed bowls and ladle the hot soup on top. The heat from the soup will wilt the leaves. Serve with warm flatbread, such as pita or naan.

This hybrid Thai coleslaw is based on the classic *som tum*, usually made from grated green papaya (when unripe, the fruit is firm, crunchy and perfect for grating). Alas, green papaya is not easy to find, so I've used red cabbage instead. The word "coleslaw" comes from *koolsla*—Dutch for cabbage salad. I merged these two classic dishes to make a salad with a delicious new twist.

thai coleslaw

To make the dressing, reserve a few cilantro leaves, then put the rest in a blender or food processor. Add the chiles, garlic, soy sauce, lime juice, and sugar and blend until smooth. Set aside.

Blanch the beans in boiling water for 2 minutes, then refresh in cold water. Mix the cabbage, beans, tomatoes, and scallions in a bowl. Pour the dressing on top, toss well to coat, and let marinate for about 30 minutes.

Spoon into bowls lined with the lettuce leaves, if using, sprinkle with the ground peanuts and the reserved cilantro leaves, then serve.

4 oz. green beans, trimmed

2 cups finely shredded red or white cabbage

3 plum tomatoes, halved lengthwise, seeded, and sliced

4 scallions, sliced

⅓ cup roasted peanuts, coarsely ground

4 cup-shaped lettuce leaves, to serve (optional)

DRESSING

a handful of fresh cilantro

2 red serrano chiles, seeded

2 garlic cloves, chopped

2 tablespoons light soy sauce

2 tablespoons freshly squeezed lime juice

2 tablespoons palm sugar or soft brown sugar

SERVES 4

grilled asparagus and leaf salad

with sesame-soy dressing

During its short season, I feast on asparagus nearly every day. I think pan-grilling is the best way of cooking the spears—it seals in their sweet, earthy flavor. Turn this salad into a main dish by adding boiled eggs.

3 tablespoons sesame seeds

2 bunches of asparagus, about 24 spears

2 tablespoons dark soy sauce

2 tablespoons balsamic vinegar

5 tablespoons olive oil, plus extra for brushing

2 cups mixed salad leaves, such as arugula, watercress, and spinach

SERVES 4–6

Lightly toast the sesame seeds in a dry skillet, stirring frequently, until golden and popping. Transfer to a bowl and let cool.

Wash the asparagus and cut off any tough stalks. Brush with olive oil. Heat a stove-top grill pan until very hot, add the asparagus (in batches, if necessary) and cook, turning occasionally, until bright green, blistered, and slightly charred, about 5–7 minutes (depending on thickness).

Put the toasted sesame seeds, soy sauce, and balsamic vinegar in a bowl and gradually whisk in the oil until emulsified. To assemble, put the salad leaves on a platter, arrange the asparagus on top, drizzle with the sesame dressing, and serve.

2 lb. new potatoes, scrubbed

4 scallions, chopped

3 tablespoons capers

$\frac{1}{2}$ cup sour cream or crème fraîche

$\frac{1}{2}$ cup low-fat plain yogurt

1 teaspoon finely grated lemon zest

$\frac{1}{2}$ teaspoon saffron strands, soaked in 1 teaspoon hot water

kosher salt or sea salt and freshly ground black pepper

snipped chives, to serve

SERVES 4–6

Cook the potatoes in boiling salted water for 15–20 minutes or until tender, then drain and let cool.

Mix the remaining ingredients in a bowl, then add the potatoes and turn until well coated. Cover and chill for at least 30 minutes to let the flavors develop. Serve sprinkled with snipped chives.

saffron potato salad

No ordinary potato salad: this one is cloaked in a luscious, creamy dressing flavored with saffron. Serve it as part of a salad feast: with Puy lentils dressed in lemon juice, onion, and herbs; and a green salad tossed in a sweet-and-sour vinaigrette.

1 romaine lettuce, outer leaves removed, or 2 small lettuce hearts

freshly grated Parmesan cheese, to serve

CROUTONS

2 thick slices white bread, cubed

1 tablespoon olive oil

DRESSING

2 eggs

¼ cup freshly grated Parmesan cheese

3 tablespoons white wine vinegar

2 teaspoons vegetarian Worcestershire sauce

1 tablespoon snipped chives (optional)

¼ cup olive oil

kosher salt or sea salt and freshly ground black pepper

SERVES 4–6

This classic salad never seems to lose its appeal and is constantly being updated. The original recipe calls for barely cooked eggs, which many vegetarians find unpalatable and should be avoided if you are pregnant, ill, very young, or elderly. Boiled eggs, cooked until the yolks are just set, make a fantastic dressing, and who needs anchovies when you can use a vegetarian Worcestershire sauce? If unavailable, add an extra pinch of salt instead.

caesar salad

To make the croutons, put the cubes of bread in a bowl, drizzle with the olive oil, and toss until evenly coated. Tip onto a baking sheet and bake in a preheated oven at 375°F until golden and crisp on all sides, about 10 minutes. Check the bread occasionally while cooking, so it doesn't burn. Let cool.

To make the dressing, put the eggs in a saucepan of cold water and bring to a boil. Cook for 5–6 minutes, then drain immediately and cool under cold running water. Peel the eggs when cold, then put in a small bowl and mash with a fork. Add the remaining dressing ingredients, except the oil, and whisk thoroughly. Gradually add the oil—a little at a time—whisking until emulsified.

Tear the lettuce into pieces and put in a large bowl, pour over the dressing, and toss until well coated. Top with the croutons, sprinkle with Parmesan, and serve.

warm chickpea salad

with spiced mushrooms

This entrée salad was inspired by Middle Eastern cuisine, where beans, yogurt, and mint are widely used. Make this dish more substantial by serving it on a bed of couscous or bulgur wheat. The convenience of canned chickpeas may appeal if you don't have time to soak and cook the dried variety. You won't notice any difference in taste.

⅔ **cup dried chickpeas or 16 oz. canned chickpeas**

3 tablespoons olive oil

12 oz. button mushrooms

2 garlic cloves, chopped

1 red serrano chile, seeded and chopped

2 teaspoons ground cumin

juice of 1 lemon

¾ **cup plain yogurt**

a large handful of mint leaves, chopped

8 oz. baby spinach leaves, about 5 cups

kosher salt or sea salt and freshly ground black pepper

SERVES 4

If using dried chickpeas, soak them overnight in cold water, then rinse and drain. Put in a saucepan, cover with water, and bring to a boil. Cook for 10 minutes, then add salt, reduce the heat, and simmer for 1–1½ hours, until tender. If using canned chickpeas, drain, rinse, and drain again.

Heat 2 tablespoons of the oil a skillet. Add the mushrooms, season with salt, and cook until softened. Reduce the heat, then add the garlic, chile, and chickpeas. Sauté for 2 minutes, then add the cumin and half the lemon juice. Cook until the juices in the skillet evaporate, then set aside.

Put the yogurt in a bowl, then add the chopped mint and the remaining lemon juice and oil. Add salt and pepper and mix until blended. Divide the spinach between 4 plates or put on a serving platter, add the chickpea and mushroom mixture, then pour the yogurt dressing over the top and serve.

2 red bell peppers,
halved and seeded

2 yellow bell peppers,
halved and seeded

1 lb. ripe plum tomatoes,
about 4 medium

¼ cup red wine vinegar

2 garlic cloves, crushed
to a paste with coarse
kosher salt or sea salt

freshly ground black
pepper

½ cup extra virgin olive
oil, plus extra for
drizzling

2 tablespoons capers

⅓ cup black olives,
pitted

1 small or ½ large loaf
day-old ciabatta, cut
coarsely into cubes

a bunch of fresh basil,
leaves, torn

SERVES 4–6

Make this sumptuous salad with flavorful, deep-red tomatoes. The bread drinks up the rich, summer flavors of the tomato and roasted pepper dressing. It's important to use a crusty, firm-crumbed bread, such as ciabatta, country-style, or sourdough, so it doesn't revert to a dough-like state.

tuscan panzanella

Put the peppers cut-side down on a baking sheet and broil until blistered and charred. Transfer to a plastic bag, seal, and let cool (the steam will loosen the skin, making it easier to peel). Scrape off the skin, then cut the peppers into strips, reserving any juice.

Halve the tomatoes and scoop out the cores and seeds over a bowl to catch the juice. Purée the cores and seeds in a blender, then press the extra juice through a strainer into the bowl. Discard the pulp and seeds. Cut the tomato halves into strips.

Put the tomato juice, vinegar, garlic, and freshly ground black pepper in a bowl. Gradually add the ½ cup extra virgin olive oil, whisking until blended.

Mix the strips of peppers and tomatoes in a bowl, add the capers, olives, ciabatta, and basil and mix. Add the dressing, toss well to coat, then set aside for 1 hour to develop the flavors. Drizzle with extra olive oil and serve.

To make the latkes, peel the potatoes, then grate on the coarse side of a box grater or in a food processor. Transfer to a strainer and let drain. Press excess moisture out of the potatoes (or they will "spit" when cooked) and put them in a bowl. Finely chop the onion and add to the bowl. Add the lemon zest and juice, flour, baking powder, and salt and mix well. Return to the strainer—liquid will continue to drain out of the mixture while you prepare to cook the latkes.

Heat about ¼-inch depth of olive oil in a skillet. Add rounded tablespoons of the mixture and flatten slightly—don't overcrowd the pan. Sauté for 2–3 minutes on each side until golden and crisp. Remove with a slotted spoon and drain on crumpled paper towels. Keep the latkes warm in the oven while you cook the rest.

To make the avocado crème, scoop the avocado flesh into a bowl and mash with a fork. Add the remaining ingredients and beat until smooth, then serve with the latkes.

NOTE: Latkes make excellent canapés. Sauté teaspoonfuls of the mixture as described above, then serve topped with the avocado crème and cilantro leaves. Makes about 50.

lemon potato latkes

with gingered avocado crème

Though rather indulgent, sautéed potato cakes are worth every wicked mouthful. Keep them small and they'll cook in a matter of minutes. Eat them as soon as possible or reheat later in a very hot oven for 5 minutes. With this spicy avocado accompaniment or one of the dipping sauces on page 59, latkes taste even better.

2 large potatoes, about 1½ lb.

1 small onion

grated zest of 1 lemon

2 teaspoons freshly squeezed lemon juice

¼ cup all-purpose flour

¼ teaspoon baking powder

1 teaspoon kosher salt or sea salt

olive oil, for cooking

GINGERED AVOCADO CRÈME

1 large ripe avocado, halved and pitted

juice of 1 lime

1–2 teaspoons finely grated fresh ginger

½ teaspoon crushed garlic

1 red serrano chile, seeded and finely chopped, or 1 tablespoon chile sauce

1 tablespoon soy sauce

2 tablespoons plain yogurt

MAKES 20–24, SERVES 4

Mix the flour, yeast, and salt in a large bowl and make a well in the center. Add 1 cup warm water and the 2 tablespoons oil. Gradually work in the flour mixture to make a soft but not sticky dough. If it is too dry or too sticky, add extra water or flour, 1 tablespoon at a time.

Invert onto a floured surface and knead thoroughly for 10 minutes, until smooth and elastic. Put in an oiled bowl and turn the dough until shiny all over. Cover with a damp cloth and let rise in a warm place until doubled in size—about 30 minutes.

Meanwhile, to make the topping, cut the onions in half, from top to bottom, and thickly slice lengthwise. Heat the oil in a skillet, add the onions, and sauté until golden. Add the salt, sugar, and wine and cook until the onions have caramelized, about 3–5 minutes.

Sprinkle the polenta or cornmeal onto a baking sheet. This will prevent the focaccia from sticking and will make the base crisp.

Punch down the risen dough with your knuckles, then transfer to the prepared baking sheet and flatten into a round, about 1 inch thick. Top with the caramelized onions and Gruyère. Cover and let rise as before for 30 minutes (no longer or the bread will be hard and dry).

Bake in a preheated oven at 425°F for 30–40 minutes, until golden. Let cool slightly, then cut into wedges and serve.

2½ cups white bread flour

1 teaspoon salt

¼ oz. package active dry yeast*

2 tablespoons olive oil, plus extra for greasing

3 tablespoons polenta or cornmeal

CHEESE AND ONION TOPPING

1 lb. red onions

2 tablespoons olive oil

a large pinch of salt

1 teaspoon sugar

¼ cup white or red wine

1 cup grated Gruyère cheese

SERVES 4–6

* To use compressed fresh yeast, crumble ½-oz. into a pitcher, mix to a smooth paste with ¼ cup warm water, then top up to 1 cup. Pour into the well in the flour, then add the 2 tablespoons oil. Proceed with the recipe.

caramelized onion and gruyère

focaccia

For a long time, I was afraid of making bread, thinking it too laborious. Then a few years ago, I made a New Year's resolution to make a loaf twice a week and in doing so overcame my fear. I find that kneading is a good stress-buster. It also keeps my arms in great shape and warms me up on a cold day. This is the simplest of loaves—almost like pizza with a lush topping. It's a meal in itself or is perfect with soup.

An explosion of flavor and texture: the crisp coating protects the deep-fried mushrooms so they are juicy, not greasy. Vary the cheese filling if you can't find dried porcini mushrooms—add a little finely chopped red chile or a mixture of chopped herbs. These balls make a terrific appetizer or delicious party food.

stuffed polenta mushrooms

32 button mushrooms, 1–2 inches diameter

½ cup polenta or cornmeal

3 tablespoons sesame seeds

1 teaspoon salt

2 eggs

sunflower oil, for sautéing

CREAM CHEESE FILLING

⅓ cup dried porcini mushrooms

¾ cup cream cheese

a handful of chives, snipped with kitchen shears

salt and freshly ground black pepper

MAKES 16, SERVES 4–6

To make the filling, pour 2 cups boiling water over the dried porcini and let soak for 20 minutes. Drain (reserving the liquid for another recipe), squeeze dry, and chop finely. Put in a bowl, add the cream cheese, chives, salt, and pepper and mix well. Set aside.

Snap the stems off the mushrooms, then slice ¼ inch off the flat side of each cap. Discard the trimmings. Mound 1–2 teaspoons of the filling into each mushroom and sandwich together to make 16 balls. Make sure the caps fit snugly together.

Mix the polenta or cornmeal, sesame seeds, and salt in a bowl. Break the eggs into a small bowl and beat. Dip 1 ball into the egg, coat well, then roll in the polenta mixture, pressing the mixture onto any uncovered area. Repeat until all the balls have been used. Chill for 15 minutes or until needed.

Heat about 1 inch depth of oil in a large skillet until hot or until a cube of bread browns in 30 seconds. Add the balls and fry for about 10 minutes until lightly golden all over. Remove with a slotted spoon and drain on crumpled paper towels. Serve hot.

Lightly grease a large skillet with 1 teaspoon of oil. Lay a tortilla flat in the pan and cover with cheese and 4 or 5 fillings of your choice. Top with a second tortilla and press down gently. Cook over a moderate heat until the bottom tortilla is golden and crisp, about 5–7 minutes. Cover with a plate, turn the pan over, and lift it off. Slide the inverted quesadilla back into the pan and cook as before. Cut into triangles.

Serve with chopped cilantro and yogurt, crème fraîche, or sour cream, if using.

VARIATION

To broil or bake the quesadillas, put a tortilla on a lightly greased baking sheet, top with cheese, preferably Cheddar, and add 4–5 fillings of your choice. Cook under a hot broiler or in a preheated oven at 350°F for 10 minutes or until the cheese is golden.

large flour tortillas, 8-inch diameter

Cheddar cheese, grated, feta cheese, crumbled, or cream cheese

sunflower oil, for greasing

FILLING, CHOOSE FROM:

chopped tomatoes

chopped scallions

chopped medium-hot red chiles, such as serrano

sliced pickled jalapeño chiles

finely sliced zucchini

sliced mushrooms

chopped bell peppers

chopped avocado

pitted black olives

mashed, canned beans such as refried, black, pinto, or borlotti beans

ground cumin

pimentón (smoked paprika)

TO SERVE (OPTIONAL)

chopped cilantro

plain yogurt, crème fraîche, or sour cream

SERVE 1 TORTILLA PER PERSON

quesadillas

You're heading for the refrigerator in search of something to demolish your small but acute appetite. You find some tomatoes, scallions, cheese, and a package of flour tortillas—and presto! Your hunger will be satisfied in less than 15 minutes. I haven't given quantities—there's no need, just pile on as much filling as you like. Fried, broiled, or baked, this Mexican snack also makes excellent party food.

topped bruschetta

Bruschetta is a fancy Italian name for toast. But I'm not talking about any old toasted bread—it has to be a crusty, open-textured loaf, such as ciabatta, sourdough, or country-style, rubbed with garlic and drizzled with olive oil. Pile high with either of these juicy toppings and serve 2 pieces per person for a stunning appetizer or 3 for a snack or light lunch.

1 ciabatta loaf or other country-style bread

1 fat garlic clove, halved crosswise

fruity extra virgin olive oil, for drizzling

SLOW-ROASTED TOMATOES

2 lb. plum tomatoes, about 10

3 garlic cloves, sliced

2 tablespoons olive oil

2 teaspoons balsamic vinegar

a pinch of sugar

kosher salt or sea salt and freshly ground black pepper

5–6 basil leaves, torn, to serve (optional)

WILD MUSHROOMS WITH APPLES AND MADEIRA

1 tablespoon butter

8 oz. mixed wild mushrooms, such as chanterelles, porcini, and oysters, or a mixture of wild and cultivated mushrooms, cleaned and sliced if large

1 Granny Smith apple, sliced

1 tablespoon freshly squeezed lemon juice

$\frac{1}{3}$ cup Madeira wine or dry sherry

$\frac{1}{3}$ cup mascarpone cheese

kosher salt or sea salt and freshly ground black pepper

chopped parsley, to serve

SERVES 4–6.

To make the bruschetta, cut the bread into slices 1 inch thick. Rub the slices all over, especially the crust, with the cut end of the garlic halves and drizzle with olive oil. Toast, grill, or char-grill until golden and toasted on both sides.

To make the tomato topping, cut the plum tomatoes in half lengthwise and put, cut side up, on a baking sheet lined with foil. Tuck in the garlic and drizzle with the olive oil and balsamic vinegar. Sprinkle with the sugar, salt, and pepper, then roast in a preheated oven at 300°F for 1½–2 hours, until the tomatoes have shrunken slightly and are golden at the edges. To serve, spoon onto the bruschetta and top with basil, if using.

To make the mushroom topping, melt the butter in a skillet, add the mushrooms, salt, and pepper, and cook until softened. Toss the apple slices in the lemon juice, then add to the skillet and sauté for 2–3 minutes. Add the Madeira or sherry and cook, stirring, until the alcohol has evaporated and the sauce has reduced slightly. Stir in the mascarpone until blended. To serve, spoon onto the bruschetta and sprinkle with chopped parsley.

spiced roasted nuts

Liven up a tossed salad or serve as party nibbles with drinks. I'm a great fan of nuts and seeds—my favorites being pumpkin seeds, which puff up impressively when roasted. Rich in iron and minerals, they are good for you, too. Mix your own selection of nuts—choose from sunflower seeds, pine nuts, cashews, macadamia nuts, pecans, Brazil nuts, and almonds.

1 tablespoon olive oil

2 teaspoons dark soy sauce

a squeeze of fresh lemon juice

a pinch of sugar

3–4 drops Tabasco sauce

½ teaspoon paprika

1 teaspoon sesame seeds

1 cup mixed raw nuts and/or seeds

MAKES 1 CUP

Put all the ingredients, except the nuts and/or seeds, in a bowl and whisk until mixed. Add the nuts and/or seeds, stir until coated, then tip onto a baking sheet and spread out in a single layer.

Roast in a preheated oven at 375°F, stirring every 2 minutes, until golden and aromatic.

Let cool, then serve or store in an airtight container until needed.

2 tablespoons butter

4 shallots or 1 onion, sliced

1 cup grated Cheddar or Gruyère cheese

⅓ cup beer

a pinch of kosher salt or sea salt

1 teaspoon mustard

2 eggs, lightly beaten

4 slices of bread

freshly ground black pepper

SERVES 2–4

rarebit

"Welsh rabbit"—also known as rarebit—is a glorified version of cheese on toast. It dates back to the mid-sixteenth century, but over time has evolved into countless variations. If you fancy a comforting snack or something light for brunch, lunch, or supper, this easy-to-make rarebit is hard to beat.

Melt the butter in a heavy-bottom saucepan, add the shallots or onion, and cook until softened. Add the cheese, beer, mustard, and salt. Stir over a low heat until the cheese has melted. Add the beaten eggs and stir until the mixture has thickened slightly, about 2–3 minutes. Don't overcook or you will end up with scrambled eggs. Toast the bread on both sides, then spoon the cheese mixture onto the toast and cook under a hot broiler, until puffed and gold-flecked. Serve with lots of black pepper.

SWEET CHILE SAUCE A great dipping sauce, especially good with wontons (page 114). Put $1/3$ cup light corn syrup, 1 tablespoon soy sauce, and 1 tablespoon rice or cider vinegar in a bowl. Add 1 sliced red serrano chile and mix well. **MAKES $1/2$ CUP**

CHILE COCONUT SAUCE For dipping or dressing stir-fried vegetables. Put $1/3$ cup coconut cream, 2 teaspoons chile paste, and 2 teaspoons freshly squeezed lime juice in a bowl and mix well. **MAKES $1/2$ CUP**

ASIAN VINAIGRETTE Perfect for noodle salads. Put 1 tablespoon dark soy sauce, 1 tablespoon sesame oil, and 1 tablespoon balsamic vinegar in a bowl and mix well. **MAKES 3 TABLESPOONS**

SOY-MAYO DRESSING Divine with potatoes or steamed vegetables. Put $1/3$ cup good-quality mayonnaise in a bowl, add 2 tablespoons dark soy sauce, and mix well. **MAKES $1/2$ CUP**

BLUE CHEESE DRESSING I A thick, creamy dressing for leafy salads. Mash 6 oz. Gorgonzola or dolcelatte cheese in a bowl. Add 3 tablespoons white wine vinegar, $1/2$ cup olive oil, salt, and pepper. Whisk until creamy and smooth. **MAKES 1 CUP**

BLUE CHEESE DRESSING II Superb with Parmesan Patties (page 104) or baked potatoes. Put 6 oz. dolcelatte or Danish Blue and 6 oz. cottage cheese in a bowl. Mash with a fork until blended. **MAKES ABOUT 1 CUP**

super-quick dressings and sauces

Strong flavors will liven up any dish—from raw or steamed vegetables to salads and grilled food. You can serve a selection of these high-speed accompaniments as dips at cocktail parties.

dips, salsas, & sauces

babaganouj

A Middle Eastern eggplant purée. Charring the eggplant over an open flame gives them a subtle smoked flavor. You can also do this on an outdoor grill or in a super-hot oven. If you are oven-roasting, halve the eggplant lengthwise, then score the flesh with a knife, drizzle with olive oil, and roast, cut side up, at 425°F until golden and softened. Peel, then follow the method in the recipe—gorgeous.

2 medium eggplant

juice of 1 lemon

1 garlic clove

2 tablespoons olive oil

2–3 tablespoons plain yogurt

salt and freshly ground black pepper

MAKES ABOUT 2 CUPS

Push a fork into the stem-end of each eggplant and lay them directly over a high gas flame. Rotate the eggplant as the skin chars and blackens and continue to roast until softened, about 15 minutes. Steam will escape when cooked.

Transfer to a plate and let cool. Peel and discard the skin. Don't worry if a few charred bits remain—this will add extra flavor. Put the peeled flesh in a food processor, add the lemon juice, garlic, olive oil, and yogurt, and blend to a purée. Add salt and pepper to taste. Alternatively, crush the garlic and put in a bowl with the peeled eggplant and other ingredients. Mash with a fork until smooth. Check the consistency: if you want a thinner dipping sauce, add more yogurt or oil, as necessary. The texture of the dip will be coarser made this way than by machine.

Serve with toasted pita bread cut into triangles and raw vegetables, such as radishes, carrots, celery, and snowpeas.

sesame yogurt dip

½ cup sesame seeds

½ cup plain yogurt

½ cup mayonnaise

2–3 tablespoons dark soy sauce

MAKES ABOUT 1½ CUPS

Crudités will disappear in no time at all if you serve them with this dip. Use also as a sauce for steamed vegetables or a nutty dressing for salads. For a well-balanced flavor, I like to use half yogurt and half mayonnaise, but you can use all mayonnaise or all yogurt, if you prefer.

Put the sesame seeds in a dry skillet and toast, stirring until lightly browned and beginning to jump around in the pan. Transfer to a bowl and let cool.

Add the yogurt, mayonnaise, and soy sauce and mix well. This dip is best eaten on the day it's made: otherwise the sesame seeds will lose their crunch.

This piquant mixture is a robust accompaniment for Breakfast Burrito (page 24), Haloumi Fajitas (page 82), and Tamales (page 84–6). It's also a splendid party dip. For grilled food, try the corn or mango variation—its sweetness complements the smoky, charred flavors of outdoor cooking.

salsa fresca

Mix all the ingredients in a bowl and set aside for about 30 minutes for the flavors to develop.

MANGO SALSA

Replace the tomatoes with 1½ cups peeled and diced fresh mango. Use chopped mint instead of the cilantro.

CORN SALSA

Instead of tomatoes, use 1½ cups corn kernels, fresh or frozen, cooked in boiling water until tender.

1½ cups ripe tomatoes, finely chopped

1 small red onion, finely chopped

2 green serrano chiles, seeded and finely chopped

juice of 2–3 limes

a small handful of cilantro, finely chopped

kosher salt or sea salt

MAKES 1½ CUPS

pickled jalapeño salsa

OK, so the tomatoes come out of a can and the chiles out of a jar, but this salsa tastes sensationally authentic and has the added benefit of staying fresh and full of flavor for at least a couple of days in the refrigerator.

1½ cups canned chopped plum tomatoes

¼ cup sliced jalapeño peppers in vinegar, drained and coarsely chopped

2 tablespoons jalapeño vinegar from the jar

1 small onion, finely chopped

a handful of cilantro, chopped

kosher salt or sea salt

MAKES 2 CUPS

Drain the tomatoes through a strainer, shaking to remove excess liquid, then discard the juice. Transfer the tomatoes to a bowl, add the remaining ingredients, and stir to mix. Set aside for 30 minutes for the flavors to develop, then serve.

thyme and mushroom gravy

Gravy is usually served with traditional English sausages and mashed potatoes. Vegetarians don't have to miss out on this classic dish as there are now many top-quality alternatives to meat sausages. Cook spicy, organic vegetarian sausages, then pile onto a bed of creamy mashed potatoes and top with gravy. Chase it all down with a glass of chilled beer.

2 tablespoons olive oil

1 onion, sliced

2 teaspoons fresh thyme leaves

1 bay leaf

1 cup coarsely chopped mushrooms

2 tablespoons all-purpose flour

½ cup port or other fortified wine

1 cup vegetable stock

2 tablespoons dark soy sauce

SERVES 4

Heat the oil in a saucepan, add the onion, and sauté until golden. Add the herbs and mushrooms and cook until softened, about 5 minutes. Sprinkle with the flour and cook, stirring, for about 2 minutes. Stir in the port or wine, vegetable stock, and soy sauce and simmer, stirring, until the gravy has thickened slightly, 3–5 minutes. Remove and discard the bay leaf. Pour the gravy into a pitcher and serve.

½ cup dried lima beans, or 16 oz. canned beans

2 large heads of Belgian endive, about 1 lb.

4 tablespoons butter

4 leeks, about 12 oz., sliced into ½-inch pieces, well washed, then drained and patted dry with paper towels

1 cup vegetable stock

1 cup port

2 tablespoons soy sauce

2 teaspoons sugar

4 sprigs of rosemary

1 bay leaf

1 small red serrano chile, seeded and chopped, or ½ teaspoon hot pepper flakes

kosher salt or sea salt and freshly ground black pepper

SMOKED CHEESE MASH

2 lb. Yukon gold potatoes, cut into small, equal pieces, about 1 inch

2 tablespoons butter

½ cup milk

1⅓ cups naturally smoked cheese, such as smoked Cheddar or smoked mozzarella, cut into cubes

kosher salt or sea salt

SERVES 4–6

If using dried lima beans, soak them overnight in cold water, then rinse and drain. Put in a saucepan, cover with water, and bring to a boil. Cook for 10 minutes, then add salt and simmer for 30 minutes, or until tender. Drain. If using canned beans, rinse and drain.

Cut the endive lengthwise into quarters, but don't trim off the base. Melt the butter in a large skillet, add the chicory, and cook, turning occasionally, until golden, about 10 minutes. Add the remaining ingredients, tucking in the rosemary and bay leaf. Bring to a boil, cover, and simmer for 15 minutes. Turn the chicory over, increase the heat, and cook for a further 10 minutes, until the leeks are tender and the gravy has thickened.

Meanwhile, cook the potatoes in salted boiling water for about 20 minutes, or until tender. Drain thoroughly and return to the pan and set it over a low heat for 1 minute to steam dry. Add the butter and milk and mash until smooth. Stir in the smoked cheese, let stand for 2 minutes, then add salt to taste.

Spoon the potatoes onto warmed plates, top with the braised chicory and bean mixture, and serve with the sauce poured over.

braised belgian endive
with beans and smoked cheese mashed potatoes

Belgian endive has a bitterness which some people find unpleasant, but others find addictive. Cooking helps reduce this taste and the flavor is balanced with the slight sweetness of the beans and aromatic gravy. Creamy mashed potatoes make this hearty meal complete.

entrées

roasted teriyaki tofu steaks

with glazed green vegetables

Dark soy sauce, sweet mirin, and dry sake make up the unique flavors of teriyaki. Add fresh or dried shiitake mushrooms to the marinade for a richer flavor. Marinating the tofu in this assertive Japanese sauce also gives it a succulent, delicate character. You can buy ready-made teriyaki sauce, but it only faintly resembles the real thing, so try to make your own—it's very easy and well worth it.

1 lb. fresh firm tofu, cut into 4 pieces

4 fresh or dried shiitake mushrooms (optional)

8 oz. fresh or dried egg noodles

TERIYAKI MARINADE

½ cup dark soy sauce

½ cup mirin (Japanese sweet rice wine)

½ cup sake

1 tablespoon sugar

GLAZED GREEN VEGETABLES

2 tablespoons sunflower oil

2 garlic cloves, finely sliced

1 cup broccoli florets or chopped broccoli rabe

1 leek, white and light green parts finely sliced

8 oz. baby bok choy, quartered lengthwise, or 2 cups chopped spinach leaves

1 fennel bulb, trimmed and finely sliced

2 teaspoons cornstarch mixed with ¼ cup cold water

TO SERVE

2 scallions, finely sliced diagonally

1 tablespoon sesame seeds, toasted in a dry skillet until golden-brown

SERVES 4

To make the marinade, put the soy sauce, mirin, sake, and sugar in a large skillet and heat, stirring until the sugar has dissolved. Add the tofu and mushrooms, if using. Simmer gently for about 15 minutes, turning the tofu over halfway through cooking.

Transfer the tofu steaks to a lightly oiled baking dish or roasting pan. Spoon a little sauce on top and roast in a preheated oven at 425°F for 10 minutes. Keep them warm. Using a slotted spoon, remove the mushrooms from the remaining sauce, squeeze dry, and slice finely. Reserve the sauce.

To make the glazed vegetables, heat a wok until hot, then add the oil. Add the garlic, broccoli, leek, and sliced mushrooms and stir-fry for 2 minutes. Add the bok choy or spinach and fennel. Stir-fry for 2 minutes. Add the reserved sauce and ¼ cup water, stir, cover, and cook for 2 minutes. Push the vegetables to the back of the wok, add the cornstarch mixture to the bubbling juices, and stir until thickened. Mix the vegetables into the sauce. Cook the noodles according to the package instructions, then drain.

To serve, put a nest of noodles on warmed plates and pile on the vegetables. Turn the tofu steaks over and put shiny side up on top of the vegetables. Sprinkle with the scallions and toasted sesame seeds and serve.

piedmontese peppers

with gorgonzola polenta

Elizabeth David first popularized Piedmontese peppers in her book *Italian Food* in 1954. There is simply no better way of stuffing peppers. Olives and capers replace the traditional anchovies, adding a slight piquancy, while sweet tomatoes and basil caramelize slowly in rich garlicky juices.

The hollowed-out peppers make an excellent container for the filling, acting like a miniature roasting pan. Serve hot, warm, or cold with broiled blue cheese polenta and arugula salad.

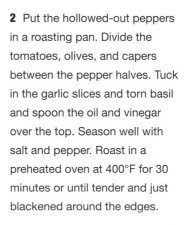

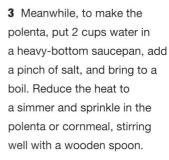

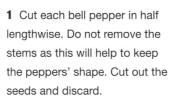

PIEDMONTESE PEPPERS

2 red bell peppers

2 ripe plum tomatoes, cut into quarters

8 black olives, pitted

1 tablespoon capers

2 garlic cloves, sliced

8 basil leaves, torn

¼ cup olive oil

2 teaspoons balsamic vinegar

kosher salt or sea salt and freshly ground black pepper

GORGONZOLA POLENTA

¾ cup polenta or coarse cornmeal

2 tablespoons butter

2oz. Gorgonzola cheese, cut into small chunks

kosher salt or sea salt (optional)

TO SERVE

arugula leaves

SERVES 2–4

1 Cut each bell pepper in half lengthwise. Do not remove the stems as this will help to keep the peppers' shape. Cut out the seeds and discard.

2 Put the hollowed-out peppers in a roasting pan. Divide the tomatoes, olives, and capers between the pepper halves. Tuck in the garlic slices and torn basil and spoon the oil and vinegar over the top. Season well with salt and pepper. Roast in a preheated oven at 400°F for 30 minutes or until tender and just blackened around the edges.

3 Meanwhile, to make the polenta, put 2 cups water in a heavy-bottom saucepan, add a pinch of salt, and bring to a boil. Reduce the heat to a simmer and sprinkle in the polenta or cornmeal, stirring well with a wooden spoon.

4 Cook, stirring, until the mixture begins to pull away from the sides of the pan, about 15–30 minutes (depending on the quality and type of polenta) or according to the package instructions. The polenta should be thick and lump-free.

5 Add the butter and salt, if needed, and stir well. (Do not overseason the polenta—the cheese is quite salty already.) Add the Gorgonzola and mix thoroughly.

6 Transfer to a shallow tray or wooden board (dampened with water to prevent sticking) and spread into an 8-inch square. Let cool until firm. The polenta can be made several hours ahead or the day before, then cooled and refrigerated until needed.

7 Cut the polenta into 4 squares, put on a nonstick baking sheet and cook under a very hot broiler until the cheese begins to bubble and melt. To serve, transfer the polenta to warmed plates, top with the bell peppers, and serve with arugula.

Pad Thai, probably the best-known of all Thai noodle dishes, takes only 5 minutes to cook. Use thick ribbon-like rice noodles ("rice sticks") for authenticity, or rice vermicelli or egg noodles. Tamarind, commonly used in Asian cooking, has a unique sour flavor, but you can substitute freshly squeezed lime juice.

pad thai noodles

Heat a wok until very hot, then add the oil. Add the eggs and noodles and stir-fry for about 2 minutes, until the eggs are lightly scrambled. Add the remaining ingredients and stir-fry for a further 3–5 minutes, until the noodles are cooked. Divide between 4 warmed bowls and serve sprinkled with the peanuts, scallions, and cilantro.

¼ **cup sunflower oil**

4 eggs, lightly beaten

6 oz. dried thick rice noodles, soaked in warm water for 5 minutes, then drained

3 cups curly kale or other leafy green, tough central core removed and leaves coarsely chopped

¼ **cup tamarind paste or 2 tablespoons freshly squeezed lime juice**

¼ **cup sweet chile sauce**

¼ **cup light soy sauce**

1 cup freshly grated carrot

1 cup bean sprouts, trimmed and rinsed

TO SERVE

⅓ **cup roasted peanuts, chopped**

4 scallions, finely sliced

cilantro leaves

SERVES 4

To make the spice paste, dry-toast the spice seeds in a skillet, shaking until they pop and turn lightly golden. Transfer to a blender or spice grinder, add the remaining ingredients and ⅓ cup water, and grind to a smooth paste. Set aside.

Roast the eggplant directly over a high gas flame until charred and softened, about 15 minutes. Alternatively, roast in a preheated oven at 425°F for about 40 minutes. Let cool, then peel and discard the skin. Don't worry if a few charred bits remain— this will add extra flavor.

Heat the oil or ghee in a large, heavy-based saucepan, add the onion, and cook until softened. Add the spice paste and stir for 2 minutes to release the aromas, then add the pepper, sweet potatoes, zucchini, and chickpeas. Cover and cook, stirring occasionally, for 10 minutes. Add the tomatoes and 1 cup water, then bring to a boil and simmer, uncovered, for about 20 minutes.

Put the peeled eggplant in a blender, add the coconut milk, and pulse to a coarse purée. Add to the pan and bring back to a simmer. Add salt, if necessary. Cook for 10 minutes, then remove from the heat, cover, and let stand for at least 30 minutes or preferably overnight.

Reheat, then serve with rice, cilantro sprigs, yogurt, and mango chutney.

charred eggplant and coconut curry

I wanted to re-create the subtle smoked flavor of Indian dishes cooked in a tandoor oven—and here is the result. Based on a charred, then puréed eggplant, this unusual curry is incredibly good. Don't be put off by the long list of ingredients for the spice paste—it's easy to make and will add a greater depth of flavor. The curry can be made in advance and, in fact, improves by being left overnight so that all the spicy flavors can develop.

1 medium eggplant, about 8 oz.

2 tablespoons vegetable oil or ghee

1 red onion, chopped

1 red bell pepper, chopped

1½ cups peeled and diced sweet potatoes, about 8 oz.

1 medium zucchini, about 8 oz.

16 oz. canned chickpeas, rinsed and drained

16 oz. canned chopped tomatoes

1 cup unsweetened coconut milk

kosher salt or sea salt, to taste

SPICE PASTE

1 tablespoon cumin seeds

1 tablespoon coriander seeds

½ teaspoon cardamom seeds, about 10 pods

½ teaspoon fenugreek seeds

2 inches fresh ginger, peeled and grated

4 garlic cloves

1 teaspoon ground turmeric

1–2 serrano chiles, seeded, or 1 teaspoon hot pepper flakes

1 tomato, quartered

2 teaspoons kosher salt or sea salt

1 teaspoon sugar

TO SERVE

steamed basmati rice

sprigs of cilantro

mango chutney

plain yogurt

SERVES 4–6

pumpkin and tofu laksa

Laksa is a Malaysian curry. It usually consists of rice noodles, crunchy raw vegetables, and fragrant herbs, bathed in a spicy coconut soup. The distinctive perfume of fresh lemongrass and kaffir lime leaves is fundamental to the spice paste and these are available from Asian food stores and markets. If you can't find these aromatics, replace them with grated lime zest and fresh lemon juice, or use a store-bought laksa paste or Thai curry paste instead, but read the label carefully—most contain ground shrimp.

8 oz. peeled, seeded butternut squash or pumpkin, cut into ¹/₂-inch cubes

10 oz. tofu, dried with paper towels and cut into 4 triangles

3²/₃ cups coconut milk

¹/₄ cup light soy sauce

2 teaspoons sugar

6 oz. rice vermicelli noodles

2¹/₂ cups bean sprouts

1 medium tomato, cut into 8 wedges

2 inches cucumber, cut into thin strips

8 sprigs of cilantro

a large handful of mint leaves

2 scallions, chopped

sunflower oil, for sautéing

SPICE PASTE

2 garlic cloves, coarsely chopped

2 red chiles, seeded and coarsely chopped

2 inches fresh ginger, peeled and finely grated

1 small onion

¹/₄ teaspoon ground turmeric

2 stalks lemongrass, sliced

4 kaffir lime leaves, chopped

SERVES 4

1 To make the spice paste, put all the ingredients and 3 tablespoons water in a blender or spice grinder and purée until smooth (add more water, if necessary).

2 Put the squash or pumpkin in a saucepan, then add salt and 2 cups water. Bring to a boil, then simmer for 10 minutes, until the cubes are tender, but still chunky. Drain, reserving the cooking liquid.

3 Heat 1 inch depth of sunflower oil in a wok or skillet. Add the tofu and sauté until golden and crisp all over. Remove with a slotted spoon and drain on crumpled paper towels. Set aside.

4 Heat 2 tablespoons of the oil in a saucepan, add the spice paste, and sauté for 2 minutes to release the aromas. Add the coconut milk, fried tofu, soy sauce, and sugar. Add the reserved pumpkin liquid. Bring to a boil, then simmer for 10 minutes.

5 Meanwhile, put the noodles in a bowl, cover with boiling water, and let soak for 5 minutes. Drain and divide between 4 warmed bowls.

6 Top with the bean sprouts, tomatoes, and cooked squash or pumpkin. Add a piece of sautéed tofu to each bowl.

7 Ladle over the hot coconut soup, top with the cucumber, cilantro, mint, and scallions, then serve.

haloumi fajitas

Fajitas—usually made with beef or chicken—are utterly delicious and can be adapted easily for vegetarians, using haloumi. This firm cheese from Cyprus is unique; it won't melt when fried and develops a delicious crisp crust. Eat the fajitas as soon as you make them; the haloumi loses tenderness if left for too long after cooking. If you can't find this cheese, use tempeh (page 10), found in the frozen section in natural food stores.

To make the marinade, put the garlic and salt in a mortar and crush to a paste with a pestle. Transfer to a bowl, add the remaining ingredients, except the oil, and whisk together. Add the oil in a steady stream, whisking until the mixture has emulsified. Put the haloumi or tempeh in a shallow dish, add enough marinade to cover, and turn until coated. Put the peppers, onions, zucchini, and mushrooms in a bowl, add the remaining marinade, and mix well. Cover both dishes and let marinate in the refrigerator for at least 30 minutes.

Stack the tortillas, wrap in foil, and put in a preheated oven at 300°F for about 15 minutes until warm. Meanwhile, heat a large skillet or wok until very hot, add the marinated vegetables and liquid, and stir-fry until the juices have evaporated and the vegetables are golden and slightly caramelized, about 20 minutes. Transfer to a heatproof dish, cover, and keep it warm in the oven.

Drain the haloumi or tempeh, discarding the marinade. Put the slices in the skillet or wok in a single layer. (If using tempeh, add 3 tablespoons olive oil to the pan.) Cook over a moderate heat for about 10 minutes, turning halfway through cooking, until golden.

Serve the tortillas, vegetables, and cheese separately, so that people can make their own fajitas. To assemble, put a warm tortilla on a plate, add a spoonful of vegetables to one half and top with haloumi or tempeh. Bring the uncovered half of the tortilla up over the filling, then tuck the corners underneath the fajitas. Serve with guacamole, salsa, and lots of sour cream, crème fraîche, or yogurt.

1 lb. haloumi cheese or tempeh, sliced

2 red onions, halved and cut into wedges

1 red bell pepper, seeded and cut into strips

1 yellow bell pepper, seeded and cut into strips

1 green bell pepper, seeded and cut into strips

1 medium or 2 small zucchini, quartered lengthwise and cut into chunks

8 oz. button mushrooms

MARINADE

2 garlic cloves

1 tablespoon coarse kosher salt or sea salt

4 limes, the grated zest of 2 and the juice of all

a handful of fresh cilantro, chopped

½ teaspoon dried oregano

½ teaspoon hot pepper flakes

1 teaspoon cumin seeds

1 teaspoon sugar

1 tablespoon white wine vinegar

½ cup dark rum

½ cup olive oil

TO SERVE

8–10 large flour tortillas, 8 inches in diameter

Guacamole (page 13)

Pickled Jalapeño Salsa or Salsa Fresca (pages 62–3)

sour cream, crème fraîche, or plain yogurt

SERVES 4–6

tamales

These simple cornmeal packages originated in ancient Mexico and are often eaten at fiestas and family celebrations. Masa harina—a special type of cornmeal—is used in the filling, then the tamales are wrapped in a corn-husk jacket before being gently steamed. (Banana leaves also make an excellent protective wrap.) The result—light, fluffy mounds.

Blue masa harina is so-called because the corn kernels are actually this color. It has the best corn flavor, but, if you can't find it, use ordinary masa harina or polenta instead. Serve with rice, refried beans, and salsa for a substantial entrée.

1 stick butter

1⅓ cups masa harina, preferably blue* or polenta

a pinch of salt

1 teaspoon baking powder

1 chipotle chile*, soaked in hot water for 20 minutes, then drained, seeded, and chopped (optional)

about ½ cup vegetable stock or water

7 oz. Cheddar cheese or Monterey Jack cheese, cut into 8 blocks, ½ x 2½ inches

8–10 dried corn husks* or 2–3 banana leaves

TO SERVE

canned refried beans

steamed white rice

Salsa Fresca (page 63)

MAKES 8, SERVES 4

* Available from specialist Latin American food stores.

1 Put the butter in a food processor and mix until light and fluffy. Add the masa harina or polenta, salt, baking powder, and chile, if using, and mix. With the machine running, slowly pour in enough stock or water through the feed tube to make a soft dough.

2 Divide the corn dough into 8 pieces and mold each one around a block of cheese until completely enclosed.

3 If using dried corn husks, soak them in boiling water for several minutes until softened, then drain and separate the layers. Wrap the tamales in a layer of husk, covering with extra bits of husk, if necessary.

4 Using thin strips of husk, tie each end of the package close to the filling to look like a Christmas cracker. Repeat until all the tamales are wrapped and tied.

5 If using banana leaves, cut 16 strips, 2½ inches wide. Put a tamale at the bottom of a strip and roll up. Wrap a second strip around the open ends to close.

6 Push a cocktail stick through the middle of the package to secure. Repeat wrapping in banana leaves and securing until all the tamales are made.

7 Put the tamales in a bamboo steamer set over a saucepan of simmering water. Steam for 1 hour. Serve the refried beans, rice, and salsa separately, so people can help themselves and unwrap their own tamales. This is the fun part!

To make the coulis, heat the olive oil in a saucepan, add the garlic and ginger, and sauté until fragrant. Add the tomatoes, vinegar, sugar, and Madeira or sherry and simmer gently for 20–30 minutes, stirring frequently. Add salt and cayenne pepper to taste. Transfer to a blender and purée until smooth. For an extra-smooth consistency, push the purée through a strainer. Set aside.

Put the trimmed spinach in a large saucepan, cover, and heat, stirring occasionally, until just wilted. Drain and let cool. Wring out in a clean cloth, then chop.

Heat the olive oil in the pan, add the onions, mushrooms, coriander, cinnamon, salt, and pepper, and cook until softened and the juices have evaporated. Add the garlic, sauté briefly, then add the chestnuts. Cook for 1–2 minutes, then add the spinach and marmalade and heat through. Season to taste.

Working with 1 sheet of phyllo at a time (keep the rest covered with a damp cloth to stop them drying out), line the prepared cake pan. Press a sheet gently into the sides of the pan and let the edges overhang. Brush with melted butter and slightly overlap with another sheet. Continue to layer and butter the sheets as before, until the pan is completely covered. Spoon in the chestnut mixture and smooth flat. Fold the overhanging phyllo in towards the center and ruffle the top so the phyllo stands in peaks. Brush with butter.

Bake in a preheated oven at 350°F for 30 minutes. Unmold carefully and slide onto a baking sheet. Return to the oven for a further 20 minutes, until golden and crisp all over. Let stand for a few minutes. Reheat the coulis. Using a serrated knife, cut the torte into wedges and serve with the coulis poured over.

chestnut, spinach, and mushroom phyllo torte

with tomato and ginger coulis

A star replacement for turkey at a vegetarian Christmas dinner or special meal—packed with fresh, spicy, rich flavors. The buttery phyllo is light and crisp, but use olive oil if you are cooking for vegans. Ready-cooked, vacuum-packed chestnuts are extremely convenient to use and the filling can be made a day in advance.

4 cups spinach leaves, well washed, with tough stalks removed

2 tablespoons olive oil

2 onions, chopped

2 cups chopped mushrooms

2 teaspoons ground coriander

2 teaspoons ground cinnamon

3 garlic cloves, chopped

1 lb. cooked, peeled chestnuts, chopped

2 heaped tablespoons thick-cut marmalade

5 sheets phyllo pastry, about 11 x 20 inches

4 tablespoons butter, melted

kosher salt or sea salt and freshly ground black pepper

TOMATO AND GINGER COULIS

⅓ cup olive oil

4 garlic cloves, chopped

2 inches fresh ginger, peeled and chopped

2 lb. canned chopped tomatoes

1 tablespoon balsamic vinegar

1 tablespoon dark brown sugar

⅔ cup Madeira wine or dry sherry

kosher salt or sea salt and cayenne pepper

9-inch springform cake pan, brushed with melted butter

SERVES 6–8

torta di risotto

with char-grilled zucchini and three cheeses

1 medium zucchini, about 8 oz., cut lengthwise into ¼-inch slices

⅓ cup olive oil

3 garlic cloves, chopped

16 oz. canned chopped plum tomatoes

½ teaspoon balsamic vinegar

1 teaspoon dark brown sugar

2 handfuls of basil, leaves torn or coarsely chopped

1 cup arborio risotto rice

4 oz. mozzarella cheese, cut into ½-inch cubes

4 oz. Fontina or other mature, hard cheese, cut into ¼-inch cubes

⅔ cup freshly grated Parmesan cheese

¼ cup toasted breadcrumbs

kosher salt or sea salt and freshly ground black pepper

9 x 5 x 3-inch loaf pan, lightly oiled

SERVES 4–6

Heat a stove-top grill pan until very hot. Brush both sides of the zucchini slices with 2 tablespoons of the oil. Add to the pan and sear, turning halfway through cooking, until softened and marked with black stripes. Alternatively, put on an oiled baking sheet, add salt and pepper, and roast in a preheated oven at 400°F for 15–20 minutes until golden.

Heat the remaining oil in a saucepan, add the garlic, and sauté until fragrant. Add the tomatoes, vinegar, sugar, salt, and pepper. Simmer for 10 minutes or until the sauce has thickened slightly. Stir in the basil.

Add the rice to a saucepan of boiling salted water (there is no need to measure the water). Bring back to a boil, then reduce the heat and simmer until the rice is tender, but still firm (al dente), about 10 minutes. Drain.

Add the rice to the tomato sauce and mix well. Stir in the cheeses and add salt and pepper, if necessary.

Sprinkle 2 tablespoons of the breadcrumbs into the prepared loaf pan, tipping the pan from side to side until coated. Spoon in half the rice mixture and smooth flat. Add the zucchini in a single layer, then top with the remaining rice. Smooth flat, pressing down firmly. Sprinkle with the remaining breadcrumbs. (The torta may be refrigerated at this point, then cooked later.)

Bake in a preheated oven at 425°F for 30–40 minutes or until golden and bubbling around the edges. Let stand for 10 minutes. Run a long-bladed, sharp knife between the torta and the pan, then turn out onto a board or platter, tap the pan all over, and lift it off. Cut the torta into slices and serve with a green salad.

Listen to the "oohs" and "aahs" as you present this dish to hungry friends. It's a totally new way of serving risotto—and the secret vegetable layer is so unexpected. I particularly like zucchini, but you can experiment with other vegetables: char-grilled eggplant, peppers, or asparagus are all delicious. Give yourself a head start—make the torta up to a day in advance, chill until needed, then let it reach room temperature before baking.

Cut the eggplant lengthwise into quarters and score the flesh with a crisscross pattern. Slice the zucchini in half lengthwise. Cut a thin slice off the bottom of the onions and cut a cross in the top. Split the chiles in half. Leave the garlic whole.

Put all the vegetables, except the tomatoes, cut side up in a roasting pan or dish. Tuck the rosemary and chiles into the onions. Reserve 2 tablespoons of oil and brush the remainder all over the vegetables. Drizzle with the lemon juice and sprinkle with salt and pepper.

Roast in a preheated oven at 400°F for 30 minutes, then brush the tomatoes with the remaining oil and put on top of the half-roasted vegetables. Cook for 15–20 minutes until the vegetables are golden and the tomatoes have split. If using cherry tomatoes, add them after 40 minutes and roast for a further 5–10 minutes.

1 medium eggplant

2 medium zucchini

4 red onions, unpeeled

2 red serrano chiles

1 whole head of garlic, unpeeled

**4 plum tomatoes
or 16 cherry tomatoes,
preferably "on the vine"**

4 sprigs of rosemary

¾ cup olive oil

juice of ½ lemon

**coarse kosher salt or
sea salt and freshly ground
black pepper**

SERVES 4

provençal roasted vegetables

Preparation is kept to a minimum and the result is a thing of beauty. Make sure you provide a side plate to put the bits on as people pluck their way through the sweet, juicy vegetables.

minted grilled zucchini

**4 medium zucchini,
about 2 lb.**

2 tablespoons olive oil

**4 teaspoons white
wine vinegar**

**a handful of mint,
leaves torn**

**kosher salt or sea salt
and freshly ground
black pepper**

SERVES 4

Perfect for a summer lunch, this Mediterranean recipe and simple char-grilling technique bring out the best in zucchini. They cook to a sensuous texture and absorb the contrasting flavors of the tangy vinegar and fragrant mint.

Trim and discard the ends off the zucchini, then cut the vegetable lengthwise into ribbon-like slices and put in a bowl. Drizzle with the olive oil and, using your hands, gently toss the slices until well coated.

Heat a stove-top grill pan or nonstick skillet until very hot. Add the zucchini ribbons (in batches, if necessary) and cook until softened and marked with black stripes on both sides. Transfer to a shallow dish and drizzle with the vinegar while the zucchini are still warm. Add salt and pepper and let cool.

Pile the zucchini ribbons into a serving bowl, sprinkle with the mint and lots of freshly ground black pepper. Serve.

12 shallots, unpeeled

8 garlic cloves, unpeeled

2 lb. orange-fleshed sweet potatoes, cut into even chunks

1 teaspoon coriander seeds, crushed

2 red serrano chiles

$\frac{1}{3}$ cup olive oil

kosher salt or sea salt and freshly ground black pepper

SERVES 4

Put the shallots and garlic in a bowl, cover with boiling water, let soak for 30 minutes, then drain and peel. The skins should slip off easily.

Transfer to a roasting pan and add the sweet potatoes, coriander seeds, and whole chiles. Add the olive oil, salt, and pepper and toss well to coat.

Roast in a preheated oven at 400°F for 30 minutes until golden and tender. Shake the pan from time to time during cooking and brush the vegetables with the pan juices.

roasted sweet potatoes

with shallots, garlic, and chiles

Crisp, golden, and bravely flavored is how I like my sweet potatoes. This recipe is for garlic and chile lovers everywhere!

lemon-roasted new potatoes

Potatoes love to be roasted. These zesty little spuds have a crisp tangy exterior and are fluffy inside. Serve with steamed greens or roasted vegetables.

2 lb. baby new potatoes, scrubbed

¼ cup olive oil

2 lemons, grated zest of both and juice of 1

1 teaspoon sugar

kosher salt or sea salt and freshly ground black pepper

SERVES 4

Cook the potatoes in salted boiling water for 5 minutes, drain, then transfer to a roasting pan.

Whisk the olive oil, lemon zest and juice, sugar, salt, and pepper in a bowl, pour over the potatoes and toss well to coat.

Roast in a preheated oven at 375°F for 20–30 minutes, turning and basting frequently with the pan juices, until golden and tender.

chile greens

with garlic crisps

I often have cravings for dark green vegetables—probably because they're rich in iron and vitamin C. The term "greens"—used loosely to describe any leafy green— includes Swiss chard, bok choy, beet greens, spinach, and much more. Many need only brief steaming or stir-frying to retain color, nutrients, and flavor. Remove any tough stalks before cooking.

1 lb. greens (see recipe introduction above)

2 tablespoons olive oil

4 garlic cloves, sliced

1 red serrano chile, seeded and finely sliced

salt and freshly ground black pepper

SERVES 4

Coarsely chop the greens, but if using bok choy, cut lengthwise into wedges. Gently heat the olive oil in a large saucepan. Add the garlic, sauté until golden and crisp, about 2–3 minutes, then remove and set aside. Add the chile to the infused oil in the pan and cook for 1 minute. Tip in the greens— they will splutter, so stand back. Add salt and pepper and mix well. Cover and cook, turning the greens occasionally using tongs, until tender: spring greens will take 5 minutes; Swiss chard, bok choy, and beet greens, about 3 minutes; and spinach about 1–2 minutes.

Transfer to a warmed serving dish and top with the garlic crisps.

VARIATION

For a festive treat, perfect at Christmas, omit the garlic and chile. Sauté ½ cup pine nuts in the oil until golden, then remove and set aside. Add the greens, the grated zest of 1 orange, and 1 teaspoon sugar and cook as described above. Serve with the pine nuts and ½ cup cranberries sprinkled on top.

Turn ordinary vegetables into something fabulous with this gorgeous Thai-flavored sauce. Use it as a marinade here, but also try it as a ketchup—on veggie burgers or on the vegetarian version of a hot dog. The sauce will keep for a week in the refrigerator.

thai-glazed vegetable skewers

Put the Thai barbecue sauce ingredients in a blender or food processor and blend until smooth.

Peel the mango with a sharp knife and stand it upright on a board, narrow end pointing up. Slice off thick cheeks parallel to the stone and cut off strips around the stone. Cut the flesh into equal chunks.

Thread the skewers with the fruit and vegetable chunks, each starting and ending with a lime leaf, if using. Brush the sauce generously over the loaded skewers, then cover and marinate in the refrigerator for at least 30 minutes. Reserve the remaining sauce.

Put on a hot outdoor grill or stove-top grill pan or under a preheated broiler and cook, turning occasionally and basting with the remaining sauce, until tender and lightly charred.

1 large, firm, ripe mango

1 yellow bell pepper, seeded and cut into 10 pieces

2 small red onions, cut into 10 wedges

2 small zucchini, cut into 10 pieces

1–2 limes, cut into 10 slices

10 button mushrooms

1 red bell pepper, seeded and cut into 10 pieces

5 serrano chiles, halved (optional)

20 kaffir lime leaves (optional)

THAI BARBECUE SAUCE

6 tablespoons coconut cream, or 3 tablespoons coconut milk powder mixed with 3 tablespoons water

⅓ cup dark soy sauce

2 tablespoons dark brown sugar

2 tablespoons rice wine vinegar or freshly squeezed lime juice

3 tablespoons tomato purée

3 kaffir lime leaves, chopped

1 stalk lemongrass, finely sliced

1–2 bird's eye chiles, sliced

1 fat garlic clove, sliced

2 tablespoons sunflower oil

10 metal or long bamboo skewers (if bamboo, soak in water for 30 minutes)

MAKES 10

vegetarian grills

feta-stuffed peppers

The stuffing is not cooked, merely heated through and is more like a warm salad than a hot filling. Roasting the peppers on an outdoor grill gives them a unique, smoky flavor and their natural sweetness combines perfectly with the tangy wheat salad.

Put the bulgur wheat in a bowl, cover with boiling water, and let stand for 30 minutes, until the grains are puffed and swollen. Drain, if necessary.

Cut the peppers in half lengthwise and remove and discard the seeds and membranes. Leave the stalk.

Put the remaining ingredients in a bowl, add the soaked bulgur, season with salt and pepper, and mix well. Pile the stuffing into the pepper halves.

Cook on a hot outdoor grill or stove-top grill pan until the peppers are tender and blackened underneath and the stuffing is warmed through. Serve with a crisp, green salad and warmed pita bread.

½ **cup bulgur wheat**

2 red, yellow, or orange bell peppers

6 oz. feta cheese, crumbled

3 handfuls of mixed fresh herbs, such as parsley, mint, dill, basil, and cilantro, chopped

1 garlic clove, crushed

2 teaspoons finely grated fresh ginger

1 tablespoon sumac or 1 tablespoon freshly squeezed lemon juice

2 tablespoons olive oil

kosher salt and freshly ground black pepper

SERVES 4

parmesan patties

Great outdoor food. Kids and grown-ups can't resist burgers and these are no exception. Make in advance to save time, then chill or freeze until needed. Oven-bake rather than grill outdoors for best results. Let's face it, you'll be popping in and out of the kitchen anyway, so these patties will leave space free on the grill for other things.

Heat the oil in a skillet, add the onions, mushrooms, thyme, and salt, and sauté until the onions are softened and golden. Let cool.

Transfer to a food processor, add the cheeses, beans, breadcrumbs, and freshly ground black pepper. Pulse until mixed, then add the soy sauce, wine, mustard, egg, and cornstarch. Process until mixed, but not too smooth.

Using wet hands, shape the mixture into 8 balls, then flatten into 1-inch thick patties. Put on the prepared baking sheet, cover with plastic wrap, and chill until firm. (At this point, you can freeze the patties, then cook from frozen when needed.)

When ready to cook, brush the tops with extra oil and bake in a preheated oven at 425°F for 25 minutes, until golden and crisp (5–10 minutes longer if cooking from frozen).

Cut the rolls in half and toast, grill, or broil lightly on one side, add the patties and your choice of accompaniments, then close up and serve.

1 tablespoon olive oil, plus extra for brushing

2 onions, chopped

4 oz. mushrooms, coarsely chopped

1 teaspoon fresh thyme leaves

½ cup coarsely grated Parmesan cheese

½ cup grated Cheddar cheese

1 cup canned borlotti or pinto beans, rinsed and drained

1 cup fresh breadcrumbs

1 tablespoon soy sauce

2 tablespoons red wine

1 teaspoon Dijon mustard

1 egg, beaten

1 tablespoon cornstarch

8 soft bread rolls

kosher salt or sea salt and freshly ground black pepper

TO SERVE (OPTIONAL)

salad leaves or arugula

sliced tomatoes

sliced red onions

tomato ketchup

mayonnaise

chile sauce

Blue Cheese Dressing II (see page 59)

MAKES ABOUT 8 PATTIES

turkish stuffed eggplant

If one vegetable could sum up Turkish cooking, it would be the eggplant. I discovered this very clever idea for stuffing whole eggplant in a Turkish cookbook and not only is the process ingenious, but it is also great fun. Use long, slender eggplant, which are perfect for hollowing out and stuffing in this way: the plump variety may take too long to cook evenly without burning. Turn the eggplant often on the grill until they are tender and the skin is deeply browned all over.

2 medium eggplant,
preferably long and thin

½ cup couscous

3 tablespoons olive oil, plus
extra for brushing

2 medium onions, chopped

4 garlic cloves, chopped

1 teaspoon ground cinnamon

1 teaspoon cumin seeds

½ cup pine nuts

6 dates, pitted and chopped

1 tablespoon orange flower
water (optional)

a handful of flat-leaf parsley,
chopped

1 medium tomato, cut in half

kosher salt or sea salt and
freshly ground black pepper

TO SERVE

plain yogurt

lemon wedges

SERVES 4

1 Using a rolling pin, gently beat the eggplant all over without breaking the skin. Massage, rolling them back and forth on a work surface until collapsed and quite flat, about 1 inch thick.

2 Make a shallow cut around the stem-ends of the eggplant, but do not cut through completely. Twist the top, then pull it off—the core should come away too. Scoop out the inside of the eggplants and coarsely chop. Set aside. Sprinkle a little salt inside the cavity, then put the eggplant, cut side down, in a colander over a bowl to drain.

3 To make the filling, put the couscous in a bowl, cover with boiling water, and let soak for 15 minutes. Drain if necessary. Fluff the grains with a fork, then set aside. Heat 2 tablespoons of the olive oil in a skillet, add the onions, chopped eggplant, and salt, and sauté until softened and golden. Add the garlic, cinnamon, and cumin and cook for 2 minutes, until fragrant.

4 Transfer to a bowl. Heat the remaining oil in the skillet and add the pine nuts. Sauté until golden, then add to the mixture, along with the dates, orange flower water, if using, parsley, and couscous. Season with salt and pepper and mix well.

5 Spoon the mixture into the eggplant, pushing it firmly into the cavities (the eggplant should resume their former shape).

6 Push half a tomato into the top of each stuffed eggplant to plug the hole. Brush lightly all over with olive oil.

7 Cook on a hot outdoor grill, turning frequently, until very tender and well browned, about 30 minutes. Slice into thick disks and serve with yogurt and lemon wedges.

NOTE: To cook in the oven, put the eggplant in a roasting pan and pour in $\frac{1}{2}$-inch depth of vegetable stock and 2 tablespoons olive oil. Cover with foil and roast in a preheated oven at 400°F for 30–40 minutes, until very tender.

These grilled mushrooms are very juicy and have a sensational texture. Use tomatoes, mozzarella, and onions that are the same diameter as the mushrooms so they fit snugly into the caps. A luxurious splash of truffle oil intensifies the earthy mushroom flavor.

stuffed flat mushrooms

with mozzarella and truffle oil

4 large portobello mushrooms

olive oil, for brushing

4 teaspoons truffle oil

4 thin onion slices, the same diameter as the mushrooms

6 oz. mozzarella, cut into 4 slices

a handful of basil leaves, 4 whole, the rest finely sliced

4 large tomato slices, the same diameter as the mushrooms

kosher salt or sea salt and freshly ground black pepper

SERVES 4

Cut the stalks out of the mushrooms and discard. Brush the caps with olive oil and put, gill side up, on a plate or tray. Season with salt and pepper and drizzle the truffle oil onto the gills.

Put a slice of onion inside the cavity of each mushroom, then layer with a slice of mozzarella, a leaf of basil, and a slice of tomato. Season with salt and pepper, sprinkle with the finely sliced basil, and drizzle with olive oil.

Cook on a hot outdoor grill for about 15 minutes (without turning), until the mushrooms have softened and shrunk slightly and the cheese has melted. Serve with ciabatta bread.

mushroom and onion marmalade tartlets

A cross between a tartlet and an open sandwich, these no-fuss party tartlets are so simple to make—there's not even any pastry to make or roll out. It doesn't matter how many tartlets I make, there never seems to be enough to go around—everyone keeps coming back for more. Serve hot for best results.

2 tablespoons olive oil

1 large onion, chopped

1½ cups finely chopped or sliced mushrooms

1 tablespoon sugar

leaves from 2–3 sprigs of thyme

12 slices medium-sliced white bread

unsalted butter, for spreading

2½ cups grated Gruyère or mature Cheddar cheese

kosher salt or sea salt and freshly ground black pepper

a 2-inch glass or plain cookie cutter

two nonstick, 12-cup bun pans or shallow muffin pans

MAKES 24

Heat the olive oil in a skillet, add the onions, and sauté until softened and lightly golden. Sprinkle the sugar on top and season with salt and pepper. Add the mushrooms and thyme and cook over a high heat until the mushrooms have softened, about 5 minutes.

Using the top of the glass or cookie cutter, stamp out circles from the bread. (The glass flattens the bread at the edges, which will make the tartlets crisper.) Lightly spread butter on one side of each circle, then use to line the pan, butter side down, and press firmly into place.

Put teaspoonfuls of the mushroom mixture in the bread cups and top with the grated cheese. Bake in a preheated oven at 425°F for about 10–15 minutes until golden and bubbling. Serve hot. Alternatively, let cool, then warm through before serving.

party food

spinach and water chestnut wontons

Fried nibbles are always a favorite at parties. These crisp, golden pockets with a light filling, dipped in a sweet, fiery sauce, will be devoured in moments. Wonton wrappers come in two sizes: 3-inch or 4-inch squares, available fresh or frozen from Asian supermarkets. For this recipe, you will need the small ones. As with all fried foods, wontons are best served as soon as they are cooked and do not reheat successfully. However, you can prepare them in advance, cover, and cook at the last minute—they'll be a huge hit.

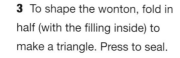

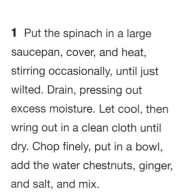

5 cups fresh spinach leaves, tough stalks removed

6 canned water chestnuts, drained and finely chopped

2 teaspoons finely grated fresh ginger

a pinch of salt

20 small wonton wrappers

1 egg, beaten

cornstarch, for dusting

sunflower oil, for frying

TO SERVE

Sweet Chile Sauce (page 59)

MAKES 20

1 Put the spinach in a large saucepan, cover, and heat, stirring occasionally, until just wilted. Drain, pressing out excess moisture. Let cool, then wring out in a clean cloth until dry. Chop finely, put in a bowl, add the water chestnuts, ginger, and salt, and mix.

2 Take the wonton wrappers out of the plastic bag, but keep them covered as you work to prevent them drying out. Put a wrapper on the work surface, brush the edges with egg and put about 1–2 teaspoons of the spinach mixture in the middle.

3 To shape the wonton, fold in half (with the filling inside) to make a triangle. Press to seal.

4 Bend the wonton into a crescent shape and bring the 2 opposite longest points together. Stick with a little egg. Repeat, filling and shaping, until all the spinach mixture has been used. Refrigerate or freeze any remaining wrappers.

5 Transfer the wontons to a plate dusted with cornstarch, turn gently until lightly coated, then shake off any excess cornstarch. (This will stop the wontons sticking together).

6 Fill a wok or large saucepan one-third full of oil and heat to 375°F. To test, drop in a piece of wonton wrapper—it will puff up immediately when the oil is at the right temperature. Add the wontons in batches of 5–6 and cook for 1–2 minutes, turning once, until puffed and golden.

7 Remove with a slotted spoon or large straining spoon and drain on crumpled paper towels. Serve hot with Sweet Chile Sauce for dipping.

mozzarella and cherry tomato skewers

A classic mix of Italian colors and flavors—in miniature. Bocconcini (meaning "little bites") are tiny balls of mozzarella. They're perfect for these skewers, but, if you can't find them, use regular mozzarella instead and cut it into 20 cubes. Choose the best olives you can find—marinated if possible.

10 cherry tomatoes, halved

20 basil leaves

10 bocconcini balls, halved, or 6 oz. regular mozzarella, cubed

20 black olives, pitted

olive oil for drizzling

kosher salt or sea salt and freshly ground black pepper

20 toothpicks

MAKES 20

Thread the tomato halves, basil leaves, bocconcini or mozzarella cubes, and olives onto the toothpicks. Lightly drizzle olive oil over the loaded skewers and season with salt and lots of black pepper. Serve.

feta and cumin phyllo packages

**3 sheets phyllo pastry, about
11 x 18 inches**

4 tablespoons unsalted butter, melted

FILLING

1 tablespoon cumin seeds

6 oz. feta cheese, finely crumbled

a handful of mint leaves, finely chopped

finely grated zest of 1 lemon

baking sheet, lightly greased

MAKES 24

Flaky, bite-size packages are quick and simple to make. Feta cheese is quite salty, so you won't need additional seasoning in these savories—only lots of cool drinks to quench your thirst. Serve Chile Coconut Sauce (page 59) for dipping.

To make the filling, dry-toast the cumin seeds in a skillet until fragrant and lightly golden. Put in a bowl, add the feta, mint, and lemon zest and mix well.

Put 1 sheet of pastry on a work surface (keep the rest covered with a damp cloth to stop them drying out) and brush with a little melted butter. Lay a second sheet on top and brush with more butter. Repeat with the final sheet.

Cut into 24 squares, about 3 inches. Put 1 teaspoon of the filling in the middle of each square, then bring the 4 corners to the center and press along the seams to seal. Dab with melted butter and cover with plastic wrap until ready to bake.

Put the phyllo parcels on the prepared baking sheet and bake in a preheated oven at 400°F for about 10 minutes, until golden. Serve warm or cold.

5 quail eggs
or 2 hen eggs

2 small heads of
Belgian endive

⅓ cup bean sprouts

¼ red bell pepper, finely
sliced lengthwise into
2-inch strips

½ cup finely sliced red
cabbage

1 scallion, finely sliced
lengthwise into 2-inch
strips

1 baby cucumber,
unpeeled, finely sliced
into strips

20 cilantro leaves

GADO-GADO DRESSING

⅓ cup smooth peanut
butter

1 tablespoon sweet
chile sauce

2 tablespoons dark
soy sauce

MAKES 20

Crisp salad leaves, such as Belgian endive and mini romaine lettuces, make wonderful edible scoops. Filled with a classic Indonesian salad, these leaf cups are a refreshing and colorful addition to any party menu. Quail eggs might have been specially invented for finger food, although they can be difficult to peel. If you can't find them, top the salad with finely chopped hard-cooked egg instead.

gado-gado salad
in Belgian endive leaves

To make the dressing, put the peanut butter in a bowl, add 2 tablespoons boiling water and, using a fork, mix quickly until the mixture is completely smooth. Stir in the chile sauce and soy sauce.

Put the eggs in a small saucepan of cold water and bring to a boil. Simmer for 3 minutes for quail eggs and 7 minutes for hen eggs. Drain immediately and cool under cold running water. Peel, then cut into quarters if using quail eggs, or chop finely if using hen eggs.

Trim the endive and separate into 20 leaves. To assemble, fill the leaves with the bean sprouts and strips of each vegetable. Using a teaspoon, drizzle the gado-gado sauce over the top, then add the cilantro leaves and quail egg quarters or chopped egg and serve.

NOTE : If you are cooking for large numbers, it may be easier and quicker to pipe the dressing over the salad. Use a piping bag fitted with ⅛-inch plain nozzle or plastic sandwich bag with the tip of a corner snipped off.

vegetarian sushi roll

Making sushi might require skill and practice, but simple
rolled sushi is very straightforward. This vegetarian
version (minus the raw fish) is a stunning canapé,
appetizer, or even a meal in itself. It's important to use
sushi rice, which cooks to the right sticky consistency.
Serve with traditional Japanese accompaniments:
sweet, pink pickled ginger and a little dish of soy sauce
for dipping. Don't forget the hot green wasabi paste,

but warn people that only a tiny
amount is needed for that fiery
horseradish sensation.

1 cup sushi rice

2–3 tablespoons Japanese rice vinegar or sushi vinegar

a pinch of salt

1 tablespoon mirin (Japanese sweet rice wine) (optional)

3–4 sheets nori seaweed

¼ firm ripe avocado, halved, pitted, and cut lengthwise into thin strips and brushed lightly with lemon juice

1 small cucumber, about 4 inches long, seeded and cut into long thin strips

½ red bell pepper, seeded and cut lengthwise into thin strips

toasted sesame seeds

TO SERVE

Japanese soy sauce

wasabi paste (hot green horseradish)

pink pickled ginger

a sushi rolling mat or heavy-duty foil

MAKES 20–30 PIECES

1 Put the rice in a strainer and wash well under cold running water until the water runs clear. Drain, let stand for at least 30 minutes, then transfer to a heavy-bottom saucepan.

2 Pour in enough water to cover the rice by 1 inch. Cover with a lid and bring to a boil, then reduce the heat and simmer for about 15 minutes until the water has been absorbed. Remove the lid, cover the pan with a clean cloth, and replace the lid. Let rest for 10 minutes.

3 Transfer the cooked rice to a large non-metal bowl. (A brown skin may have formed around the pan: simply scrape the rice away from it.) Add the vinegar, salt, and mirin, if using, and mix. For perfect sticky rice, stand it near an electric fan, stirring the rice until cooled.

4 To make the sushi rolls, toast the nori over a very low gas flame or electric hotplate for a few seconds until crisp, then put, shiny side down, on the mat or foil. Using wet fingers, put a handful of rice in the center of the nori and spread it over the top, leaving a 1 inch band uncovered nearest to you. Using the back of your finger, press a shallow groove down the middle of the rice.

5 Lay 1–2 strips of the avocado, cucumber, and bell pepper in the groove (do not overfill or you will have difficulty rolling up the sushi). Lightly sprinkle with the toasted sesame seeds.

6 Roll the mat or foil, starting from the front edge and rolling away from you, so that the rice and filling are enclosed in the nori. Dampen the edge of the nori if it doesn't stick once rolled. Remove the rolled sushi and put, join side down, in a flat container while you make the remaining rolls in the same way.

7 Using a sharp knife dipped in hot water, trim and discard the ends, then cut the roll into ½-inch thick pieces. Serve with soy sauce, pink pickled ginger, and wasabi. The sushi can be made several hours in advance, left whole, wrapped in plastic and left in a cool place until needed, but do eat on the day of making.

chocolate banana cheesecake

Chocolate and banana are natural partners in this luxuriously wicked cheesecake. Mascarpone makes the dessert lighter by reducing the cloying texture of the cream cheese.

BISCUIT BASE

8 oz. plain chocolate Milano cookies

4 tablespoons unsalted butter, melted

2 tablespoons unsweetened cocoa powder

CHEESECAKE FILLING

1 lb. cream cheese

10 oz. mascarpone cheese

2 large ripe bananas, broken into chunks

2 teaspoons pure vanilla extract

1 cup sugar

2 eggs, lightly beaten

TOPPING

4 oz. bittersweet chocolate, chopped

4 tablespoons unsalted butter, cut into cubes

1 large banana

juice of ½ lemon

9-inch springform cake pan, greased

SERVES 8–10

Crush the cookies in a food processor, then transfer to a bowl. Pour in the melted butter, add the cocoa, and mix well. Tip the crumbs into the prepared pan and press firmly with the back of a spoon or your fingertips. Bake in a preheated oven at 350°F for about 10 minutes. Let cool. Reduce the oven temperature to 300°F.

To make the filling, put the cheeses in a food processor and blend until smooth. Add the bananas, vanilla, and sugar and mix well. Add the eggs, a little at a time, and pulse until smooth. Alternatively, beat the ingredients, as above, in a bowl until smooth. Pour into the pan and bake for 30–40 minutes, until just set but still slightly wobbly in the middle (it will set firmer as it cools). Let cool in the pan, then chill for at least 3 hours or overnight.

To make the topping, melt the chocolate and butter in a heatproof bowl set over a saucepan of simmering water.

Unmold the cheesecake, but don't remove the bottom of the pan— the cookie base may break. Transfer to a serving plate. Top with the chocolate mixture and spread, letting it dribble over the edge. Cut the banana diagonally into long slices, toss in the lemon juice to prevent the pieces discoloring, pat dry, then arrange in a circle on top of the cheesecake. Chill until the topping is set. Serve.

sweet things

carrot and olive oil cake

Fruity olive oil makes this carrot cake like no other. Deliciously moist and lightly spiced, it couldn't be easier to make: you don't even need a mixer.

1 cup olive oil

2½ cups sugar

4 eggs, beaten

1⅔ cups all-purpose flour

2 teaspoons baking powder

2 teaspoons baking soda

2 teaspoons ground cinnamon

1 teaspoon ground cloves

1 teaspoon ground cardamom (optional)

1 teaspoon sea salt

1 cup coarsely chopped pecans or walnuts

1 lb. carrots, peeled and grated, about 3½ cups

MASCARPONE FROSTING

1¼ sticks unsalted butter, softened

2 teaspoons pure vanilla extract

1 cup mascarpone cheese or cream cheese

2 cups confectioner's sugar

9-inch springform cake pan, base-lined with wax paper, greased and lightly dusted with flour

SERVES 8–10

Put the olive oil, sugar, and eggs in a bowl and stir until well mixed. Sift the flour and other dry ingredients into a second bowl and make a well in the center. Add the egg and oil mixture and mix thoroughly until blended. Add the pecan or walnuts and carrots and mix well.

Pour into the prepared cake pan and bake in a preheated oven at 325°F for 1 hour 20 minutes, until a skewer inserted into the center comes out clean. Let cool in the pan, then run a knife around the edge of the cake to loosen and turn out.

To make the frosting, mix the butter, vanilla, and mascarpone or cream cheese in a food processor or bowl. Gradually add the confectioner's sugar and mix until smooth and creamy. Do not overmix or the frosting may curdle. Spread onto the cake and make patterns in the top.

white chocolate mousse torte

This no-bake dessert is not for the faint-hearted. You will only be able to manage a slender slice, but, believe me, it's all you need. I've had varying results with this recipe. Sometimes the texture is mousse-like, other times like truffles, but it's always divine. Serve after dinner with strong black coffee.

COOKIE BASE

about 30 amaretti cookies

1 stick unsalted butter, melted

MOUSSE

14 oz. white chocolate

2 cups heavy cream, at room temperature

¼ cup milk, at room temperature

9-inch springform cake pan, greased and lined with a collar of waxed paper

SERVES 12

Crush the amaretti cookies in a food processor until they look like fine crumbs, then transfer to a bowl and mix in the melted butter. Tip the mixture into the prepared cake pan and press firmly over the base with the back of a spoon or your fingertips.

Break the chocolate into pieces and melt in a heatproof bowl set over a saucepan of simmering water. Set aside and let cool until lukewarm.

Put the cream and milk in a bowl and, using an electric hand-held mixer, beat until the mixture leaves a ribbon-like trail on the surface when the mixer is lifted out of the bowl.

Using a large metal spoon, stir a spoonful of the whipped cream mixture into the chocolate to slacken, then immediately pour it into the remaining cream mixture. Stir vigorously until smooth and mousse-like. Don't worry if there are tiny lumps of chocolate flecked in the mixture— it will still taste delicious.

Pour into the prepared pan and swirl the top. Cover and refrigerate for at least 4 hours or overnight. When set, remove the pan, but leave the base on and peel off the paper collar. Let stand for a few minutes to soften, then cut into thin slices and serve.

raspberry roulade

Pure indulgence is a crisp meringue with a soft, marshmallow center, filled with whipped cream and topped with berries. Once mastered, you'll discover that a meringue is one of the simplest, prettiest, and most versatile of all desserts. You can use the basic recipe to make individual shells, then fill with lemon curd, cream, and seasonal fruit. Shells bake in a cool oven at 250°F for 45 minutes. Here I've used the meringue to make a feather-light roulade, which cooks in just 17 minutes. Sharp-flavored fruits, such as raspberries, balance the sweetness of the meringue, though you could use any of your favorite fruits.

MERINGUE

6 egg whites, at room temperature

a pinch of salt

2 cups superfine sugar

2 teaspoons cornstarch

1 teaspoon white wine vinegar

RASPBERRY ROSE FILLING

2 cups heavy cream

3–6 tablespoons rose water

2 cups raspberries

cookie sheet lined with wax paper
extra wax paper

SERVES 8–10

1 Put the egg whites and salt in a scrupulously clean, dry bowl and, using an electric hand-held mixer, whisk until stiff peaks form. (Take care: if there is any trace of egg yolk or moisture in the bowl the whites won't whisk properly.)

2 Sprinkle in 1 tablespoon of sugar at a time and whisk between each addition until the meringue is thick and glossy. Add the cornstarch and vinegar and whisk until mixed.

3 Transfer to the prepared cookie sheet and, using a spatula, spread the meringue into a rectangle about 12 x 16 inches. Smooth the surface. Bake in a preheated oven at 350°F for 17 minutes or until barely crisp. Let cool.

4 To turn out the meringue, cover with the extra sheet of wax paper, then quickly but carefully invert the cookie sheet onto the work surface. Lift off the sheet, then gently peel off the wax paper from the meringue.

5 To make the filling, put the cream and rose water in a bowl and whip lightly until softly peaking. Spoon onto the meringue and spread, leaving a ½-inch border clear all round. Add the raspberries.

6 Lift up the side of the wax paper nearest to you and use it to help roll up the roulade lengthwise. Peel back the paper as you go. Before you reach the end, carefully lift the roulade (still on the paper) onto a platter or board.

7 Roll the roulade off the paper so that the join is underneath, then slice into 8–10 pieces and serve.

Bright gelatins wobbling on a plate are a childhood favorite, but here are two delicious grown-up versions that you just have to try. Gelatin, though it may look and taste innocent, is not suitable for vegetarians. Luckily, there is a vegetarian alternative derived from seaweed, available from natural food stores.

gelatins and mousses

champagne gelatin

¾ **cup blueberries**

¾ **cup small seedless red grapes**

2 cups champagne or sparkling wine

¼ **cup superfine sugar**

3 teaspoons vegetarian gelatin (agar agar)

SERVES 4

Divide the blueberries and red grapes between 4 tall glasses or champagne flutes. Pour half the champagne or sparkling wine into a saucepan and add the sugar and gelatin. Heat gently, stirring until the sugar and gelatin have dissolved, then heat until almost boiling.

Slowly add the remaining champagne. Pour into the glasses and chill for 3 hours or until softly set. Serve immediately—the gelatin will soften as it nears room temperature.

thai coconut mousse

1 cup milk

2 stalks lemongrass, sliced

2 kaffir lime leaves, coarsely chopped

1 inch fresh ginger, unpeeled and sliced

1 small red bird's eye chile, halved lengthwise

1 can coconut milk, about 1¾ cups

⅔ **cup superfine sugar**

3 teaspoons vegetarian gelatin (agar agar)

honey-roasted peanuts, chopped, to serve

SERVES 4

Put the milk, lemongrass, lime leaves, ginger, and chile in a saucepan, bring to a boil, and simmer for 15 minutes. Let cool.

Strain the infused milk into a pitcher and add enough coconut milk to make up to 2 cups. Discard the flavorings and reserve the remaining coconut milk for another use. Return the infused milk to the pan and, using an electric hand-held mixer, beat in the sugar and gelatin until dissolved. Heat gently, beating continuously, until almost boiling, then transfer to a pitcher (for easy pouring).

Pour into 4 glass bowls. Let cool, then chill for 3 hours or until set. To serve, sprinkle with chopped peanuts.

An elegant dessert that can be made well ahead of time. For a special occasion, it's nice to stuff the pears, but, if the long list of ingredients and preparation put you off, then just omit this part. Simply serve the poached pears whole with the luscious syrup spooned over.

mulled wine pears

with spiced stuffing

4 firm, ripe pears

1 vanilla bean, split in half lengthwise

1 cup freshly squeezed orange juice

2 cups red wine

½ cup sugar

grated zest of 2 lemons

6 whole cloves

1 cinnamon stick

sour cream or crème fraîche, to serve

SPICED STUFFING

½ cup hazelnuts

1 tablespoon dark brown sugar

2 tablespoons raisins

1 teaspoon ground cinnamon

½ teaspoon ground cloves

a large pinch of freshly grated nutmeg

1½ tablespoons orange flower water

a large pinch of salt

SERVES 4

Peel the pears, leaving the stems intact. Cut a thin slice off the bottom of each one, so they stand upright, and scoop out the cores with a teaspoon. Scrape the seeds from the vanilla bean into a large saucepan, then add the bean and the orange juice, red wine, sugar, lemon zest, cloves, and cinnamon. Bring to a boil, stirring until the sugar has dissolved. Gently lower the pears on their side into the pan and simmer, turning frequently in the poaching liquid, for 30 minutes, until tender (depending on ripeness).

Using a slotted spoon, remove the pears from the poaching liquid and set aside to cool. Strain the liquid and return to the pan. Heat until reduced and syrupy. Let cool.

To make the stuffing, roast the hazelnuts in a preheated oven at 400°F for 5 minutes, until lightly golden. Let cool. Put in a food processor, pulse until ground, then add the remaining ingredients and pulse until mixed. Spoon the mixture into the hollowed-out poached pears and spread a thin layer on the bottom of each one (this will help the pears stand upright when you put them on the plates). Serve with the syrup poured over and a dollop of sour cream or crème fraîche.

2 sticks unsalted butter

1 cup raw sugar

⅔ cup honey

4 cups rolled oats

⅓ cup chopped nuts, dried fruits, or glacé ginger, or unsweetened desiccated coconut (optional)

a 8 x 12 inch shallow cake pan, greased

MAKES 12

Put the butter, sugar, and honey in a saucepan and heat, stirring occasionally, until the butter has melted and the sugar has dissolved. Add the oats and nuts, dried fruit, glacé ginger, or coconut, if using, and mix well.

Transfer the oat mixture to the prepared cake pan and spread to about 1 inch thick. Smooth the surface with the back of a spoon. Bake in a preheated oven at 350°F for 15–20 minutes, until lightly golden around the edges, but still slightly soft in the middle.

Let cool in the pan, then turn out and cut into squares.

honey oat bars

These wonderful chewy oat bars are practically effortless to make. You don't have to be an expert baker to have a go. Oat bars are perfect teatime treats or mid-morning snacks. They also travel well—wrap for a picnic or packed lunch.

chocolate chunk nut cookies

Simple to make, absolutely divine taste, crisp on the outside, soft and gooey in the middle—what more could you ask for? Vary the nuts to suit yourself: I'm fond of pecans, macadamias, and pine nuts, but you can use walnuts or hazelnuts. Keep the chocolate and nuts chunky for maximum impact.

1 cup all-purpose flour

½ teaspoon baking powder

½ teaspoon salt

1¼ sticks unsalted butter, softened

½ cup dark brown sugar

1 teaspoon pure vanilla extract

1 egg

8 oz. bittersweet chocolate, coarsely chopped

⅓ cup coarsely chopped nuts, such as pecans or hazelnuts

a large baking sheet, lined with wax paper

MAKES 12–14

Put all the ingredients, except the chocolate and nuts, in a food processor and blend until mixed. Stir in the chocolate and nuts. Alternatively, sift the flour, baking powder and salt into a bowl. Put the butter, sugar, and vanilla in another bowl and beat with a wooden spoon or electric mixer, until light and fluffy. Gradually beat in the egg. Fold in the flour mixture. Mix in the chocolate and nuts.

Scrape the cookie dough onto a large square of plastic wrap and roll into a 12-inch long sausage shape. Twist the ends to seal and chill for at least 30 minutes or until firm.

When ready to bake, unwrap the dough and cut into 1-inch thick slices. Put 1 inch apart on the prepared baking sheet (in batches, if necessary) and bake in a preheated oven at 375°F for 15–20 minutes, until just golden. Transfer to a wire rack to cool.

menu ideas

JAPANESE LUNCH

Vegetarian sushi roll

Japanese omelet

Grilled asparagus and leaf salad with sesame-soy dressing

THAI SUPPER

Thai coleslaw

Pad Thai noodles

Thai coconut mousses

LIGHT MIDDLE EASTERN LUNCH

Babaganouj with warm flatbread

Warm chickpea salad with spiced mushrooms

A FEAST FOR THE EYES

(a particularly beautiful but not too complicated meal)

Pumpkin and tofu laksa

Raspberry roulade

SUMMER SALAD FEAST

Saffron potato salad

Tuscan panzanella

Minted grilled zucchini

Green salad with blue cheese dressing I

MEXICAN INDIAN SUMMER SUPPER

Mexican gazpacho

Haloumi fajitas

Chocolate banana cheesecake

BARBECUE I

Parmesan patties

Feta-stuffed peppers

Thai-glazed vegetable skewers

Caesar salad

BARBECUE II

Turkish stuffed eggplant

Stuffed flat mushrooms with mozzarella and truffle oil

Thai-glazed vegetable skewers

Grilled asparagus and leaf salad with sesame-soy dressing

MEXICAN ALL-YEAR SUPPER OR LUNCH

Quesadillas

Tamales

Chocolate banana cheesecake

WARMING WINTER DINNER

Shiitake and field mushroom soup with Madeira and thyme

Braised Belgian endive and beans with smoked cheese mash

Raspberry roulade

DEEP-HEAT WINTER LUNCH

Lemon-potato latkes with gingered avocado crème

Charred eggplant and coconut curry

Carrot and olive oil cake

SIMPLE WINTER LUNCH

Caramelized onion and Gruyère focaccia

Lentil, coconut, and wilted spinach soup

ITALIAN DINNER WITH POLENTA IN TWO GUISES

Stuffed polenta mushrooms

Piedmontese peppers with gorgonzola polenta

VEGETARIAN CHRISTMAS I

Celeriac, saffron, and orange soup

Chestnut, spinach, and mushroom phyllo torte

Lemon-roasted new potatoes

Greens with pine nuts and redcurrants (see Chile greens with crispy garlic)

Mulled wine pears with spiced stuffing

VEGETARIAN CHRISTMAS II

Bruschetta with wild mushrooms and apples in a creamy Madeira sauce

Torta di risotto with three cheeses

Chile greens with crispy garlic

Roasted sweet potatoes with shallots, garlic, and chiles

White chocolate mousse torte

CHRISTMAS DRINKS PARTY

Mushroom and onion marmalade tartlets

Spinach and water chestnut wontons

Lemon potato latkes with gingered avocado crème

Spiced roasted nuts

Stuffed polenta mushrooms

SUMMER DRINKS PARTY

Vegetarian sushi roll

Mozzarella and cherry tomato skewers

Feta and cumin phyllo parcels

Crudités with sesame yogurt dip

Topped Bruschetta with slow-roasted tomatoes

A LUNCH OF SMALL COURSES

Babaganouj and sesame yogurt dip with warm flatbread

Topped bruschetta with wild mushrooms

Piedmontese peppers

Champagne gelatins

FUSS-FREE AUTUMN DINNER

Shiitake and field mushroom soup with Madeira and thyme

Vegetarian sausages and mashed potatoes with thyme and mushroom gravy

Provençal roasted vegetables

Raspberry roulade

FULL-ON BRUNCH BUFFET FOR 14

Cottage cheese pancakes with berries, jelly, and crème fraîche

Japanese omelet with grilled tomatoes and avocado

Breakfast burritos

Corn muffins

Caesar salad

Honey oat bars

Chocolate chunk nut cookies

index

WEIGHTS AND MEASURES: CONVERSION CHARTS

Weights and measures have been rounded up or down slightly to make measuring easier.

VOLUME EQUIVALENTS

American	Metric	Imperial
1 teaspoon	5 ml	
1 tablespoon	15 ml	
¼ cup	60 ml	2 fl.oz.
⅓ cup	75 ml	2½ fl.oz.
½ cup	125 ml	4 fl.oz.
⅔ cup	150 ml	5 fl.oz. (¼ pint)
¾ cup	175 ml	6 fl.oz.
1 cup	250 ml	8 fl.oz.

WEIGHT EQUIVALENTS

Imperial	Metric
1 oz.	25 g
2 oz.	50 g
3 oz.	75 g
4 oz.	125 g
5 oz.	150 g
6 oz.	175 g
7 oz.	200 g
8 oz. (½ lb.)	250 g
9 oz.	275 g
10 oz.	300 g
11 oz.	325 g
12 oz.	375 g
13 oz.	400 g
14 oz.	425 g
15 oz.	475 g
16 oz. (1 lb.)	500 g
2 1b.	1 kg

MEASUREMENTS

inches	cm
¼ inch	5 mm
½ inch	1 cm
¾ inch	1.5 cm
1 inch	2.5 cm
2 inches	5 cm
3 inches	7 cm
4 inches	10 cm
5 inches	12 cm
6 inches	15 cm
7 inches	18 cm
8 inches	20 cm
9 inches	23 cm
10 inches	25 cm
11 inches	28 cm
12 inches	30 cm

OVEN TEMPERATURES

110°C	(225°F)	Gas ¼
120°C	(250°F)	Gas ½
140°C	(275°F)	Gas 1
150°C	(300°F)	Gas 2
160°C	(325°F)	Gas 3
180°C	(350°F)	Gas 4
190°C	(375°F)	Gas 5
200°C	(400°F)	Gas 6
220°C	(425°F)	Gas 7
230°C	(450°F)	Gas 8
240°C	(475°F)	Gas 9